Crypto For The Curious Modern Investors

Crypto For The Curious Modern Investors

Two Voices, One City: A Fresh Take on Cryptocurrency For Skeptics and Open Minds

J.K.A.A.

Copyright © 2024 by J.K.A.A.

All rights reserved.

No part of this book may be reproduced, stored in a retrieval system, or transmitted in any form or by any means, electronic, mechanical, photocopying, recording, or otherwise, without the prior written permission of the author, except for brief excerpts used in reviews.

For permission requests, please contact:

anonvibe@yahoo.com

ISBN: 9798346296096

Disclaimer

Let's get something straight upfront: I'm not a financial advisor whispering investment secrets in your ear. This book is here to spark curiosity about cryptocurrency, not to stand in for professional guidance. If you're looking for personalized financial advice, reach out to a licensed professional who can tailor a plan to fit your goals and risk tolerance.

It's important to consider that even the most well-intentioned sources, myself included, can have unconscious biases. I'm not always right, and I encourage you to think for yourself. And remember, things in crypto can shift by the time you're reading this.

When I mention specific cryptocurrencies or exchanges, it's not a buy signal, nor is it a recommendation. I get the excitement around crypto, but caution is always key. Sometimes, a specific cryptocurrency or exchange may simply serve as an example for the topic at hand. Bottom line: don't buy something just because you see it mentioned here. Do your own independent research.

Dedication

For my parents, wife, and son.

Preface

The idea for the book struck me because I've seen firsthand how confusing and intimidating cryptocurrency can be for newcomers. People often approach crypto with a mix of curiosity and skepticism, but once they try to dive in, they're hit with a tidal wave of jargon, complex concepts, and sometimes even misinformation. It reminded me so much of my own journey—those moments of feeling completely lost and having to sift through mountains of information just to make sense of how it all works. I know I'm not the only one who has felt that way.

Recently, I read a book that managed to break down a complicated topic using a really friendly, conversational style. It wasn't even about crypto—something completely different, actually—but the way it simplified everything and made it feel approachable was eye-opening. I finished it thinking, "Wow, I finally get this." And that's when I had my lightbulb moment: if I were to write a book on crypto, why not use that same accessible, down-to-earth approach? It could make the learning curve less intimidating and, hopefully, make crypto less of a mystery for readers who are curious but overwhelmed.

So here I am, diving into the conversations between Bob and Alice about cryptocurrency. Through their back-and-forth chats, I want you to see the real struggle of tackling tough questions and exploring different viewpoints on this topic. Their discussions are like a mini version of the big conversations we're all having about money and cryptocurrency today. I've woven in a lot of my own thoughts, some of which might be controversial. But I wanted to stay true to my perspective. If you're just starting with crypto, exploring different perspectives can be really helpful. Otherwise, it's easy to get swept up in the noise and hype.

PREFACE

I chose the names Bob and Alice for my characters because they're kind of like the 'everyman' in the blockchain world. If you've read anything about crypto, you've probably come across these names as placeholders in discussions about transactions and cryptography. They're relatable and bring a sense of familiarity to the conversation.

Here's how this book is set up:

In the first part, we'll tackle how to break free from the usual ways of thinking about money. One big roadblock people hit with crypto is thinking it doesn't make sense just because it's not like regular money—for starters, it's not issued by a government. And that alone can feel pretty weird, right? A friend once asked me, "What even *is* cryptocurrency, and why does it have any value?" That's the million-dollar question, and I'm guessing it's crossed your mind, too. So, we'll dive in, exploring what crypto really is and what makes it valuable.

We'll also get into some of the stories and promises that make crypto so intriguing to its fans—the big ideas that keep people hooked. You've probably heard people say that crypto is fast, cheap, and maybe even the future of money. But, of course, it's not that simple. We'll dig past the hype and get real about some of the downsides, too. It's easy to go along with the crowd when you're only hearing the good stuff, but a closer look gives a fuller picture—the good and the not-so-great.

I've also added a section that questions whether the entire crypto space might be tied up in the sunk cost fallacy. It's a thought that keeps coming up for me, and it's worth considering.

In part two, we'll get a little more technical, covering things like blockchain basics, irreversibility, mining, consensus mechanisms, and decentralization. I've done my best to keep it simple, with plenty of analogies to make things clearer. And this isn't a formal lesson—there are already tons of resources for that. Instead, think of it as a way to go a little deeper, to look past the surface and start asking the questions that aren't always covered in a quick online search. Really, it's about testing these ideas and seeing if they stand up.

Take your time with this part, too. Settle in, grab a coffee, and start poking at the details. Don't rush—ask questions and if something doesn't sit right, go ahead and research to get the answers.

In part three, we'll dig into a variety of topics: the future of Bitcoin and crypto, the rifts within the crypto community, and things like DeFi, CEX, DEX, and many more. But it's not just a list of definitions—we'll get into how these things work and why they matter.

Expect plenty of discussions that go beyond surface-level stuff. This part aims to get you thinking about the crypto world—its potential, its problems, and what the future could hold.

At the end of the day, I hope this book sparks your curiosity, gets you thinking, and empowers you to navigate the world of crypto with confidence.

And here's what I tell my friends and family: investing should feel right for you. If crypto doesn't click, there's no shame in stepping back. In fact, this book might just be your secret weapon against overenthusiastic crypto evangelists or that FOMO-fueled advice. Everyone's financial journey is different, so saying 'no' to crypto could be one of the most informed choices you make.

Prologue

Alice stepped off the plane and felt a jolt of anticipation. Tokyo. It wasn't just a city to her; it was the heartbeat of mysteries she wanted to explore, starting with a collapse—the Mt. Gox exchange. Years ago, it had held the promise of a digital revolution before vanishing, dragging thousands of people's trust down with it. She came here with questions she hadn't yet been able to answer, looking for what the ruins of that story might tell her about the future of money.

Somewhere across the city, Bob—a longtime expat who had lived here for years—was about to stumble into an unexpected conversation. Years spent immersed in crypto had made him a self-taught advocate, but he knew it was still a divisive topic, often sparking more questions than answers. He wasn't one to push his views on anyone, but he would be lying if he said he wasn't passionate about it.

Neither of them knew that their paths would soon cross. But in a city alive with movement, sometimes, all it took was one conversation with the right stranger to start unraveling mysteries and shaping new ones.

Contents

Preface

Prologue

Part One 1

    Trust 9

    Potentials 33

    Fallacy 57

Part Two 69

    Technology 71

    Rules 87

    Challenges 131

Part Three 143

    Community 151

    Practicality 163

    Future 189

Epilogue

Afterword

Author Biography

Part One

Warm sunlight streamed through the window of a bustling Shibuya café, casting a warm glow on Bob's table in the heart of Tokyo. He sat engrossed in a brand new copy of *Digital Gold* by Nathaniel Popper, its crisp pages hinting at a recent purchase. A worn leather keychain dangled from his jeans, a small, silver Bitcoin symbol glinting subtly beneath the café lights. This detail, only noticeable to a fellow cryptocurrency enthusiast, hinted at the hidden depths of his passion.

Years spent navigating the vibrant streets of Shibuya, a microcosm of Tokyo's frenetic energy, had subtly reshaped Bob. Here, a quiet confidence held more weight than boisterous pronouncements. A comfortable silence between strangers wasn't awkward but rather a form of polite respect. The metropolis, with its unique blend of ancient traditions and cutting-edge technology, had woven itself into the fabric of his being, not through imitation, but through a deeper understanding of its cultural nuances. Tokyo, a place where history and innovation collided at every corner, had become more than just a home for Bob; it was an inspiration.

Suddenly, a startled gasp shattered the peaceful scene. Bob looked up, startled by the noise. Across from him sat a young woman, the epitome of a tourist on an adventure. Her age was hard to pinpoint – somewhere between the carefree confidence of her early twenties and the seasoned curiosity of her late twenties. Sun-kissed blonde highlights, a souvenir from a previous beach trip perhaps, contrasted with her deep blue eyes that sparkled with a mix of surprise and dismay. A well-worn backpack, overflowing with a colorful scarf and a crumpled map, sat at her feet, bearing the marks of countless journeys. Her practical outfit – jeans and a comfortable t-shirt – spoke of both a desire for ease of movement and a casual, independent style.

The source of the commotion became clear as Bob took a closer look. On her table lay a well-worn travel guide, its open page filled with colorful pictures and notes scribbled in English. Beside it, an overturned mug had unleashed a wave of green liquid, soaking both the guide and a flyer depicting a majestic temple. The spilled matcha latte threatened to spill over the edge, creating a growing mess. The woman, clearly flustered, was fumbling with a damp napkin, trying in vain to contain the green tide.

Bob rose from his chair, his initial surprise giving way to a mix of amusement and concern. The disarray of napkins, the drenched travel guide, and the woman's frantic attempts to clean up were both endearing and slightly comical. He empathized with her predicament, though.

Hesitantly, Bob considered how to help without being intrusive. The woman sighed in defeat, tossing a crumpled napkin onto the mess. Muttering in frustration, she glanced at her soaked travel guide, worry etched on her face.

Seeing her struggle, Bob silently reached for a clean napkin and offered it to her with a gentle smile. Her eyes widened in surprise before a hesitant smile played on her lips. Relief flickered across her face for a moment before she surprised him with a grateful, "Arigato gozaimashita." Her tone conveyed gratitude tinged with reservation, as if unsure about conversing further in Japanese.

The slight lilt in her voice, the scribbled notes in English, and her overall appearance all pointed to one conclusion – she wasn't a native Japanese speaker.

Taking a chance, "no worries at all," Bob replied in clear English. "Looks like you've got quite the adventure planned."

Taken aback, she replied, "Oh! You speak English?" Her tone relaxed considerably.

Bob smiled warmly. "Yes, I do. I've been living in Tokyo for a while now, but I'm originally from the States."

She nodded thoughtfully. "Ah, that makes sense. I assumed you were local because you seem so at ease here."

Bob chuckled as he continued the valiant effort to clean up the spill. Despite his efforts, a faint stickiness lingered on the tabletop. "There we go," he said with a sigh, gesturing to the now-damp and slightly sticky surface. "That should be all the renegade matcha for now. At least it's not a complete disaster zone anymore."

"Thank you so much," she said sincerely. Her earlier panic had vanished, replaced by genuine appreciation. "I was really worried about my travel guide. It's a bit worse for the wear, but hopefully I can still salvage it."

Bob peered at the damp travel guide, its cover depicting a bustling Tokyo street scene. "Looks like it's seen its share of adventures," he replied with a smile. "By the way, I'm Bob. What's your name?"

"Alice," she replied, offering a hesitant hand towards Bob. The smile that played on her lips didn't quite reach her eyes. A self-conscious glance flickered down to her hand, now thankfully free of the worst of the matcha but still slightly tacky. "This whole thing was such a disaster, but you saved the day – and maybe my travel plans."

Bob noticed the slight hesitation in her handshake and the quick glance down at her palm, which still held a trace of the matcha mishap. With a warm smile that crinkled the corners of his eyes, he took her hand in his. Despite the faint stickiness, his grip was firm and friendly. "No worries, Alice," he said reassuringly. "Disasters happen. Besides," he added with a wink, "a little matcha residue never hurt anyone."

"Actually," he continued, gesturing towards his table, "it seems your table might end up a little sticky with all that spilled goodness. Besides, these chairs here seem a bit lonely. Would you care to join me? We can move your things over, of course."

Alice glanced at the empty seats, a flicker of hesitation crossing her face before a small smile played on her lips. "Actually, I wouldn't mind that at all, Bob. Thanks for the offer." She carefully gathered her belongings and moved them to Bob's table.

"Excuse me for a moment, though," she added with a sheepish grin. "This whole matcha incident… well, let's just say my hands could use a good wash."

"No worries, Alice," Bob reassured her. "Take your time. I'll keep an eye on our salvaged travel guide here."

Once she stepped away, he glanced down at his own book, momentarily tempted to continue reading. The story of Bitcoin and the inside story of the misfits and millionaires trying to reinvent the money was fascinating, and he was eager to see what happened next.

But then, a smile tugged at his lips. The day had taken an unexpected turn, and a far more interesting story was unfolding right in front of him. He gently closed the book, placing it face down on the table. Now with his full attention on Alice, he waited patiently.

Moments later, Alice returned, a much relieved smile on her face. Her hair, now damp at the edges from hastily washing her hands, still held a trace of the earlier chaos.

Her eyes widened in surprise as she spotted a steaming mug on the table beside her empty seat. It was a matcha latte, a perfect green swirl topped with a dusting of powdered milk.

"Oh my goodness, Bob!" she exclaimed, her voice laced with disbelief and a touch of awe. "You didn't have to do that!" She paused. "But…anyway, thank you, this is so kind of you." Carefully, she picked up the mug. The warmth radiating through the ceramic was comforting against her chilled hands.

Bob chuckled. "Think of it as a peace offering," he said, "and a friendly bribe to ensure the matcha stays contained this time around." He winked playfully. "Besides, good company deserves a good drink, even if it means tempting fate with another matcha latte."

"Consider the bribe accepted," she replied. "And the matcha mishaps? Definitely a learning experience. I promise to be extra cautious this time – pinky swear?" she added, extending a finger towards him with a playful grin.

Bob grinned back, accepting her pinky swear with a gentle touch. "Deal. Now, where were we in your Tokyo adventure plans?" he asked, gesturing towards the travel guide.

Alice's smile faltered slightly. "Actually," she began, a touch of hesitation creeping into her voice, "that's a good question. I haven't gotten very far with planning yet."

Bob raised an eyebrow in surprise. "Really? Most tourists have a list of places they want to see before they even arrive in Tokyo."

"Well, you see," she mumbled, "there's a bit of a reason I'm in Tokyo. It's not exactly your typical sightseeing trip." Alice avoided touching the damp travel guide, instead nervously clasping her hands in her lap.

Intrigued, Bob leaned forward slightly. "Not your typical trip, huh? Care to elaborate?"

Alice took a deep breath, then blurted out. "There was this whole thing many years back... something called Mt. Gox, right? It all sounded so crazy."

Bob blinked, momentarily taken aback by her unexpected answer. "Mt. Gox? You know about that?" Intrigued by this young woman's seemingly random knowledge.

A hint of self-consciousness immediately crept into Alice's voice. "Don't get me wrong," she mumbled, her gaze dropping momentarily, "I barely understand crypto. But back home, everyone seems obsessed with it. So, I figured a pilgrimage to the birthplace of Mt. Gox might be a good place to start learning, right?"

A slow smile spread across Bob's face. This wasn't the typical conversation starter he expected, but something about Alice's genuine curiosity piqued his interest. Her question, though seemingly random, held an unexpected spark.

"Well, Alice," he began, taking a sip of his latte, "Mt. Gox was a big deal, indeed. A massive event that shook the Bitcoin world years ago." He paused, his gaze flickering to Alice for a moment. "Though, to be honest, it's also a big part of the reason I'm here in Tokyo."

Alice's eyes widened a fraction. This casual stranger, seemingly knowledgeable about crypto, also had a connection to Mt. Gox? "Really?" she asked, a hint of excitement bubbling beneath her polite tone. "That's fascinating! So, you're well-versed in all this cryptocurrency stuff?" she asked, curiosity piqued.

"I've picked up quite a bit over the years," Bob admitted, his tone carrying a hint of invitation. "If you want, I have the entire afternoon free. We could delve into crypto if you're curious."

Alice hadn't expected Bob's offer, but it sparked something in her. She had been curious about crypto for a while but hadn't found anyone who could really help her make sense of it. Bob's unexpected willingness to guide her through it made her wonder what had prompted the offer. Was it just casual interest on his part, or was there something deeper behind his knowledge? Her curiosity got the best of her, and with a playful smile, she asked, "I've got to know— am I about to get this crash course from someone with a hidden passion for crypto, or is there more to this story?"

Bob chuckled, a low rumble that sent a pleasant warmth through Alice. "No hidden passions here," he asserted, a hint of amusement twinkling in his eyes. "In fact, working with cryptocurrency solutions is a core part of my day-to-day responsibilities here in Japan with my current employer. That, coupled with the field's rapid evolution and potential for innovation, has naturally captured my interest."

"I see. So, Bob, how did Mt. Gox bring you to Tokyo then?" She asked.

Bob's expression grew thoughtful as he traced the rim of his cup with his finger. "After the collapse of Mt. Gox, there was a surge of interest in improving security and trust in the crypto space. I was a programmer working on a project related to blockchain technology back home, and it caught the attention of a startup here in Tokyo. They offered me a position, and I couldn't resist the opportunity to be at the forefront of such a dynamic field, all while experiencing the rich culture that Tokyo embodies."

Alice's admiration shone through her eyes. "That sounds like an incredible journey, Bob. It must be fascinating to be at the forefront of something so innovative."

Bob's smile widened. "It definitely is. Every day brings new puzzles to solve and possibilities to explore. And Tokyo itself is such an inspiring city."

As they talked, the café's background noise seemed to melt away. They were lost in their conversation, each captivated by the unexpected connection they had formed.

Bob's playful grin returned. "You mentioned Mt. Gox piqued your interest. But what specifically drew you to cryptocurrency, Alice?"

Alice met his gaze, a mixture of nervousness and excitement sparkling in her eyes. "Honestly," she began, taking a deep breath, "fresh out of college, everyone seems fascinated by this whole 'crypto' thing. Bitcoin, Ethereum – all these terms get thrown around, but no one ever explains what it's all about. It feels like everyone's getting rich quick, or at least that's what they're making it seem like on social media. But is it all just hype, or is there something real there?"

She continued. "So, here I am, practically in the shadow of the once-mighty Mt. Gox, with a very basic question…"

Bob leaned forward, showing his eagerness to hear her.

"Basic questions are the best place to start," he assured her gently.

Alice blushed a touch, momentarily embarrassed by her lack of knowledge. "So," she whispered, mindful of the café's quiet atmosphere, "what exactly is Bitcoin and cryptocurrency all about?"

Bob's smile widened, crinkling the corners of his eyes. "Cryptocurrency, eh?" he said, leaning back in his chair with a nonchalant air. "Don't worry, it's not as complex as it sounds. Think of it as just two words put together: 'crypto' and 'currency.'"

"So, break it down for a complete beginner like me," she pleaded.

Bob grinned. "The term 'currency' simply means the everyday forms of money we use, like yen, dollars, or euros. The key difference is that cryptocurrency takes a different form - it exists entirely in digital form. No physical bills or coins to carry around."

He held up a finger. "Now, the 'crypto' part of the term refers to a special technology called *cryptography*. Imagine this technology as a super-secure lock that keeps your money safe from thieves. Banks use similar security measures, but cryptography takes it a step further."

"So, putting the pieces together," Bob continued, "*cryptocurrency* essentially means a digital form of money which relies on a technology called cryptography. It's like having a secure, digital piggy bank that you can access anywhere in the world."

Trust

Alice took a thoughtful sip of her matcha latte, processing this new information. "A digital piggy bank with a super lock, huh?" she mused, a hint of somewhat understanding replacing her initial confusion. "Okay, can you actually use cryptocurrency to buy things in stores, or is it just for online stuff? It seems different from regular money."

"That's a great question, Alice. You can certainly use some of them to buy things online, and some stores are starting to accept them as well, though it's not quite as widespread as regular money yet. But there's a key difference between crypto and regular money. Now, imagine a digital money that's not controlled by any government or bank—Bitcoin is the pioneer of that," he explained, leaning back in his chair.

Bob's explanation immediately sparked a flicker of thrill in her eyes. "But isn't that risky?" she countered, a note of concern creeping into her voice. "I mean, if it's not backed by a government or regulated by a central bank, how do we know it's not just a scam?"

Now, here was the real Alice, the curious one who craved knowledge beyond the basic explanation.

Bob anticipated this question, a thoughtful smile playing on his lips. "That's a fantastic point, Alice. It's a common concern for people new to cryptocurrency. But have you ever stopped to think why we trust government-backed money in the first place?"

Alice puffed out her chest, a confident smile spreading across her face. "Why do we trust government-backed money, Bob? That's an easy one!" she declared with pride. "I mean, I majored in finance, so I should know this stuff. Here's my answer: people trust it because it's backed by the government. They control the economy, regulate the banks, and ensure the money has value. They print it, manage inflation, and... well, they make sure everything stays stable. And most importantly, it's what we use to buy things every day. The government makes sure the whole system stays together. And everyone just... knows it works." Her voice was steady, almost rehearsed, as if she was reciting something she had learned in school.

For a brief second, Alice's smile lingered, but as she spoke, her eyes drifted slightly, and her voice softened just a little.

Bob leaned forward, noticing the shift in her expression. "Hold on a second, Alice," he said gently. "You started off sounding so confident, and now you look like you're wrestling with a particularly stubborn math problem. What's going on?"

Alice sighed, like a deflated balloon. "It's strange, Bob. I thought I knew why we trusted this money everyone uses, but the more I try to explain it, the less sense it makes. It's like being on a hamster wheel – I keep going around and around, but I never get anywhere."

"A hamster wheel, huh?" Bob chuckled, a hint of amusement softening his voice. "I see what you mean. You started with a simple question, but the deeper you dig, the more complex it all seems."

Slumping back in her chair. "Sure, I use cash every day, and the government seems important, but why exactly do I trust those bills in my wallet? It's like trying to explain why the sky is blue – it just…is, right? You see, I trust government-backed money because we use it in our daily lives. But then, it's the government that makes us use their money in the first place." Her words hung in the air as if she were trying to make sense of it all.

She continued. "So, using money because it's trusted, and trusting it because it's used? It's like explaining a dream – you can describe it, but the core reason feels slippery."

She paused dramatically, leaning forward with a furrowed brow. "Moreover, why are those reasons enough? I mean, sure, the government controls it, but how do I know they're doing a good job? Suddenly, those reasons start to feel a little flimsy, you know?"

Bob chuckled softly, his eyes twinkling. "Sometimes the most fundamental things can be the trickiest to explain. It's not a bad thing, Alice. It just means you're starting to think critically about something you've always taken for granted. But hey, don't worry about that hamster wheel feeling. Consider me your personal money maze escape artist. We'll untangle this thing together, one step at a time."

Alice's lips curved into a small smile. "An escape artist, huh? Sounds promising. Alright, Bob, lay it on me. So, why do we trust government-backed money?"

Bob, leaning forward with a confident smile. "Government-backed money is, well, issued by the government. But let's take a step back. Does merely issuing something automatically give it value, or is there something more at play?"

He reached into his pocket and pulled out a 1,000 yen note. "Let's take this bill, for example. It's just a piece of paper with some ink on it, right?" He gestured to her matcha latte cup. "You go to a coffee shop, order your latte, and hand over a similar piece of paper with a picture on it. The barista accepts it without question, but why?"

Alice furrowed her brow. "Because... it's money?"

Noticing Alice's lingering uncertainty, Bob leaned in slightly, lowering his voice as if letting her in on a secret. "But why do we treat that piece of paper like it's money?" he asked, his tone soft but pointed. "What gives it value?" His eyes held hers for a moment before he continued. "It's not the paper or the metal that matters. Those things are practically worthless on their own. The value isn't in the materials—it's in something else entirely."

Alice's eyes widened as she listened intently.

Bob built on his point. "Imagine a concert ticket. The physical ticket itself, whether paper, plastic, or metal, has minimal value on its own. Its real worth lies in granting you entry to the concert. Similarly, money, whether bills, cards, or coins, derives its value not from the material but because the government requires us to use it for taxes and fees, and businesses accept it because everyone else does. If you and I are stranded on a deserted island, would those dollar bills in your wallet have any value?"

Alice shook her head firmly. "Absolutely not. They would be useless for buying anything."

Bob nodded, making it clear he was on the same page. "So it really comes down to something called *trust*. We trust the government to back up the currency and keep it steady. And we trust that others will accept it as payment. It's this whole web of trust that makes regular money work. But that trust is built on things like promises, allegiance, convenience, and past experiences. In fact, these days, most government money isn't backed by anything physical. It's more about agreeing that this piece of paper, or those numbers in your account, actually mean something."

He leaned in a bit closer, as if to share a bit of insight. "This trust is built over time and through systems we all rely on, like the banks and governments. They make sure everything is working as it should, and that helps keep the value stable. So, while it might seem like just a piece of paper or some digital numbers, it's the trust and agreements between people that really give money its worth."

"So, money's value is essentially the outcome of a giant game of trust?" Alice intrigued by this new perspective. "But what if that trust breaks down?" a thoughtful expression creeping onto her face. "What if people lose faith in the government or the money?"

Bob nodded grimly. "It's important to remember, that trust can be fragile. History is filled with examples of that happening," he said. "Financial crisis, currency collapse, government default, hyperinflation – these all stem from a breakdown in trust. When people lose faith in the value of their money, the whole system starts to crumble."

Alice tapped her chin thoughtfully, her eyes narrowing in contemplation. "So, when we pay for something with cash, we're not just paying with money, we're paying with our trust in the government?"

"Exactly!" Bob said, a triumphant grin spreading across his face. "That's the key point. So, circling back to the question of why we trust government-backed money in the first place. The answer, Alice, is way simpler than you might think. The fact that we can use it for daily purchases is the result, not the cause. We trust it because, well, we've been conditioned to, in a way like a snowball rolling downhill, gathering momentum as it goes. "

Alice was clearly intrigued. "A snowball, huh? Interesting analogy."

"Think about it," Bob continued. "First, governments establish a legal framework that mandates using their currency for taxes and fees, effectively making it *legal tender*, which means it must be accepted as payment for debts. This creates a basic level of acceptance."

"Okay, I get that," Alice said, nodding.

"Then," Bob went on, "convenience comes into play. Everyone else is using this money, so it becomes the easiest way to buy and sell things. The network effect takes hold, and trust grows incrementally. Over time, this constant exposure builds a sense of comfort and 'artificial' trust. It becomes the norm, the default, and questioning it might seem strange."

Alice frowned, her brow furrowing in thought. "But wait, Bob," she interjected, chewing on her bottom lip. "Even if it's the government, banks, and widespread use that build our trust in money, isn't that how any good system should function? I mean, if everything's set up to make us trust the currency and it works well, isn't that a positive thing? Why is there a problem with it?"

Bob stroked his chin thoughtfully. "That's a great question, Alice. Trusting the government to manage money can offer certain conveniences and benefits. But the issue isn't just about trusting the government to manage money; it's about putting our faith in them without questioning their actions. This can be dangerous because governments are prone to manipulation and may not always act in the best interests of the people. While it's convenient to rely on government-managed money, we need to be aware of the risks involved. There's a lot of blame-shifting going on: the people blaming the government for excessive money printing and spending, and the government blaming the people for being too demanding."

Bob continued, "I'm sure you've heard people talking about how printing too much money leads to inflation, right? While that's a straight forward concern, it's way more complicated than that. At its core, it's really about supply and demand."

"Let's say the government prints money and gives it out to stimulate the economy—people will naturally spend it, maybe on things like food. If demand increases faster than supply can keep up, prices will rise, and suddenly, your money buys less."

"Likewise, excessive money printing can lead to a loss of confidence in our currency on the foreign exchange market, likely causing its value to depreciate. When a country prints a lot of extra money, people can start losing confidence in it because suddenly, there's way more money out there without anything new to back it up—no increase in goods, services, or economic output. So, the money itself starts to lose its power to buy things. Foreign investors see this happening and think, 'This currency isn't as stable as it used to be,' so they pull back. When the currency drops on the foreign exchange market, its value goes down even more. And that's when things can really spiral, because a weaker currency makes imported raw materials for manufacturing more expensive, which, in turn, will drive up the cost of finished goods sold locally."

"The kicker? Even when production costs drop or demand goes down, businesses rarely lower prices because they're now enjoying higher profit margins—and they often blame inflation for it. Now, that's the kind of inflation most people are talking about."

He paused, letting the thought settle before adding, "And here's what a lot of people don't consider: inflation isn't just about price increases. It's also about *quality* and *quantity*. Think about it— whether it's a washing machine or a smartphone, they barely last a few years now, and you end up having to replace them more often. And have you noticed how food packages are getting smaller while prices stay the same? The bag of chips that used to be full now has more air than chips. You're paying the same or even more but getting less. It's not just that prices are going up; the quality and quantity of what you're buying are going down. In the past, things were built to last, and packages were filled to the brim. Now, companies use cheaper materials, or they shrink product sizes while charging the same or even more. So, when people say inflation is only 2% or 3% a year, they're missing part of the story. Are you getting the same value for your money? Most people aren't. That's inflation too. My point is that inflation is much worse than the numbers suggest."

He sighed, leaning back. "You know, sometimes I think the whole 'money printing causes inflation' thing is a narrative the government is pretty comfortable with. It gives people something easy to blame, so they don't look too closely at other things that are actually driving up prices. Stuff like poorly managed supply chains, red tape, or even bad government spending decisions. Those things don't get nearly the same attention. It's just simpler for people to point to printing money, but really, inflation's a way bigger and messier issue than that. At the core of it all is the government's apparent failure to manage the currency in a way that meets people's fair expectations. And honestly, many people can already tell that they're either exhausted of solutions or simply prefer to focus on other priorities."

Bob's expression grew more thoughtful. "So, Alice, how do you feel about the current state of the economy?"

Alice's shoulders slumped slightly. "Honestly, Bob, not great. Everything seems to be getting absurdly expensive – groceries, rent, even that new book I wanted."

"Exactly," Bob said, leaning forward. "That's what a lot of people are experiencing right now. It's a feeling of unease, a sense that something isn't quite right with the current system. Wouldn't you agree?"

Alice stared off into the distance, her eyes unfocused but intent, considering Bob's question. She thought about the constant news headlines about inflation, the rising cost of living, wages aren't keeping pace, and the struggles of her friends and family to make ends meet. A slow nod escaped her lips. "Yeah, Bob," she admitted. "I guess you have a point. Maybe the way things are being managed right now isn't working for everyone."

"Exactly, Alice. All those economic reports and theories have their place, sure, but the real measure of a system is how it impacts people's daily lives. Inflation may look like a simple percentage on paper, but it feels very different depending on what you buy. If essentials like groceries or gas spike in price, it hits hard, even if the official inflation number seems low. When the cost of living keeps rising and people are struggling to make ends meet, that says something powerful about the state of things. And right now, it's pointing to a system that probably needs more than just a minor fix."

"And no, I'm not here to just blame the government—it's not like that will solve things overnight. But I can tell you this: people are frustrated, they feel let down, and it's clear the government is running out of ways to patch things up. That's why it's dangerous to put blind trust in any system or authority, especially when that trust feels manufactured. I think it's time to put more trust back in the hands of the people."

Alice thought about it for a moment, crossing her arms as she mulled it over. "But how? How do we take the trust back?"

"It's about showing people alternatives. The more folks realize they don't have to depend on just one system—government, banks—the more trust shifts back to individuals. That's how you start taking it back, by understanding you don't have to hand over all your trust in the first place. It's not some magic fix, but it begins with being informed, knowing you have options."

"Bob, it sounds like you're suggesting cryptocurrency is this alternative you're talking about, right? But even then, it's still about trust, isn't it?" She tilted her head, her fingers tapping thoughtfully against the table. "Nothing works without trust. If regular money has value because we trust the government, aren't you just saying that cryptocurrency relies on a different kind of trust? It's the same thing, just with a different system backing it, no?"

Bob grinned and said. "Yes and no. It's a different way of thinking about trust altogether."

"Both traditional money and cryptocurrencies depend on trust to have value," he explained. "But the kind of trust is what sets them apart. With traditional money, the trust is kind of artificial, a forced and synthetic one. We use it because we have to, for taxes and stuff. It's like a system that works because everyone is kind of following the rules out of fear of punishment or even jail terms."

He continued, "I would prefer a more natural, voluntary kind of trust. People choose to trust because the system is designed in a way that you don't need to trust any one person or bank to create value. You're essentially trusting a *trustless* system, which is why I say the answer is both yes and no."

Alice frowned, her brow furrowing at Bob's words. "Wait, 'trustless?' That sounds like you're saying the system isn't worthy of trust. Like it's shady or unreliable."

Bob smiled, understanding her confusion. "Yeah, the term can be misleading. When I say 'trustless,' I don't mean untrustworthy. It means the system is set up so you don't have to rely on any single person, bank, or entity to make it work."

"It might sound strange," he continued, "that a system can be based on trust while also not trusting anyone in particular, almost as if treating everyone as inherently untrustworthy and malicious. But hear me out."

"Think about it this way," Bob continued. "Trusting people can be risky. People can make mistakes, or even cheat. What if we designed a system that didn't rely on anyone being perfect? A system that could function even if nobody could be trusted completely. Wouldn't that be a strong and innovative idea?"

Alice was intrigued, but still unsure. "I understand you're excited about this concept, Bob," she said. "But if I can be totally honest with you, it sounds like a pipe dream. I'm not sure it's actually realistic at all."

"Pipe dream, huh?" Bob chuckled. He pointed to that small Bitcoin symbol on his keychain.

Alice's eyes lit up with understanding. "So, you're saying Bitcoin is this 'trustless' system you've been talking about?"

Bob grinned. "Actually not just Bitcoin but the idea behind cryptocurrencies in general. Some people might say cryptocurrencies have no real value, but I disagree. The very idea that they can function as a trustless financial system—that alone is their inherent value. As more and more people see this system working and growing, that trust builds over time, giving it even more value."

Alice looked at Bob, impressed by his conviction. "So, you are saying this trust in cryptocurrencies, it grows 'naturally,' based on the system itself, not because anyone forces you to believe in it?"

"Precisely," Bob said. "That's what I call *organic trust*. It's not manufactured or enforced. The more people use cryptocurrencies and see their potential, the stronger this organic trust becomes."

"Organic trust," Alice repeated thoughtfully.

Bob gestured towards the gold necklace Alice was wearing, its shine catching the light from a nearby window. "Now, speaking of value," he said, "take this gold necklace, for instance. It's beautiful, no doubt. But does it have inherent value just because it's gold?"

Alice's hand instinctively went to the necklace. "Well, of course it is. Gold is precious, used in jewelry, electronics... it's a valuable metal."

Bob chuckled. "Think about it this way. Millions of years ago, gold was just another shiny rock buried underground. It wasn't inherently valuable. But over time, humans started to appreciate its beauty, its rarity. They used it for decoration, then currency. This collective trust, built over centuries, is what gives gold its value today."

Alice's brow furrowed. "So, you're suggesting that the value of gold is more like... an unspoken agreement?"

"More like a carefully constructed narrative," Bob said. "And that narrative is powerful. It's why dethroning gold as a global reserve currency would be such a seismic shift. It would challenge a deeply ingrained belief system, a system that benefits a select few."

"Like a conspiracy of the wealthy?" Alice whispered, a hint of suspicion in her voice.

"Maybe not a conspiracy in the traditional sense," Bob mindful of his words, "but definitely a system that favors those who control the narrative. Financial institutions, media, even governments all play a part in reinforcing the idea of gold's value. It's a system that works for and against them at the same time, but it's important to understand how it works, and that value itself can be influenced and even manipulated over time. It's a taboo topic, almost."

Alice looked down at her necklace, its golden sheen now seeming less certain. "So, value can be built, but also shaped by powerful forces. And it can change too?"

Bob nodded thoughtfully. "Exactly. It's less about what something *is* and more about what we *agree* it's worth. Value isn't just some fixed thing; it's shaped by consensus and belief—and often by those with the power to influence that belief. In a way, the world 'conspires' to agree on the value of something—whether that's gold, a currency, or even crypto. It's a shared belief, shaped by powerful forces, and yeah, it can change over time. That's why in that sense, trust matters as much as anything tangible."

He continued. "Gold, for instance, has value because we've all agreed it does for thousands of years. If tomorrow, people decided it was no different from iron, its worth would plummet. The same goes for currency—it's only valuable because we trust that it is. But that trust? It's delicate. A shift in sentiment, a loss of confidence, and it can all come crashing down."

Alice let out a slow breath, her mind racing. "It's strange to think that something so solid as gold, or even the money we use, could be so... dependent on belief. I thought value was just... well, there."

Bob nodded, understanding her surprise. "It's a complex world out there, Alice. The key is to keep questioning, keep learning, and don't be afraid to peel back the layers behind what we're told is valuable. And sometimes, questioning those values can lead to exciting new possibilities, just like cryptocurrencies challenging the traditional system of value, offering a new way to redefine trust and value," He winked.

Alice, still a hint of hesitant agreement in her eyes. "That's a lot to take in, Bob," she admitted. "The whole idea of a currency existing outside of a government system that challenges the way we think about trust and value...it's quite different from anything I've encountered before."

Bob wasn't surprised. This cautious acceptance mirrored his own experience. He vividly recalled the first time a close friend, eyes gleaming with a mix of excitement and bewilderment, had tried to explain to him the world of cryptocurrency. Back then, that same idea had seemed outlandish. He had been just as skeptical, the conversation teetering on the edge of a full-blown argument.

Recognizing the echo of his own past in Alice's expression, Bob decided to take a gentler approach. He gestured towards the now empty matcha latte cup. "Think about it this way. Just a few decades ago, the idea of paying for a coffee with a few taps on your phone would have seemed far-fetched. Now, it's commonplace."

A thoughtful expression settled on Alice's face. Bob's analogy clearly resonated with her. Perhaps cryptocurrency wasn't so peculiar after all. It was a seed planted, waiting to see if it would take root in her curiosity, preparing this young lady for intimacy with a new kind of money.

The aroma of freshly baked pastries wafted past Alice's nose, momentarily distracting her from the conversation. Her gaze drifted towards the counter, where a golden mountain of croissants beckoned with a flaky promise of buttery goodness.

"Mmmm," she sighed, glancing at Bob. "Those croissants look incredible. Do you think they have any almond ones?"

"Hmm, maybe? There's only one way to find out, right?" He gave her a quick smile. "How about I go check and grab one for each of us? My treat."

Alice's eyes lit up. "Really? That would be amazing, Bob. Thanks!"

With a playful nod, Bob rose from his chair. "Consider it done. Be back in a jiffy." He snaked his way through the lunchtime crowd, disappearing towards the counter.

Alice, a contented smile gracing her lips, took another sip of her matcha latte. The café's lively hum washed over her, and she felt a comfortable warmth settle in. It was just then, as she reached for her phone to check the news, that a headline caught her eye: "Bitcoin Surges – Market in Frenzy!" A spark of curiosity ignited within her.

Just as she was about to tap on the article, Bob reappeared, a triumphant grin plastered on his face and two flaky croissants nestled in a paper bag each.

"Fresh out of almond," he announced, setting a golden pastry in front of her.

Alice accepted the croissant with a grateful smile. "Thank you, Bob. You're a lifesaver."

Taking a bite, she couldn't help but let out a satisfied sigh. The buttery layers melted in her mouth, momentarily pushing the news alert from her mind.

"So," Bob began, unwrapping his own croissant, "something catch your eye on your phone? You looked intrigued."

Alice's mind buzzed with curiosity as she glanced back at the headline. "Actually, it was this article about Bitcoin," she said, her interest piqued. "It looks like the price is all over the place."

Bob's eyes widened with amusement. "Ah, price! Now that's a subject that can inspire some lively conversation."

The buttery flakes of the croissant danced on Alice's tongue as she chewed thoughtfully. Politely covering her mouth with a napkin, she asked. "But why, Bob? Why would anyone be willing to pay a high price for something without even a government guaranteeing its value?"

Bob, mid-bite of his own croissant, stopped and chuckled. "There you go again, Alice," he said, wiping a stray bit of pastry from his chin. "Stuck in the comfort zone of what you know about money. That's the thing with new ideas like cryptocurrency - our brains are wired to cling to the familiar. Cash, banks, government control - it's what we've always known, so anything different simply defies imagination."

Alice, a touch defensive, set her croissant down. "But Bob, isn't that a valid point still? Everyone agrees the value of a dollar because the government says so. Without that, wouldn't cryptocurrency just be...worthless?"

"Well, to crack the code," Bob conceded, taking a dramatic bite of his croissant, scattering flakes like confetti, "we got to take a time warp trip! It all began with the real OG of cryptocurrencies, the one and only… Bitcoin!" His eyes sparkled with enthusiasm, punctuating his words with a theatrical flair that hinted at his passion for the topic.

He continued. "Alice, Bitcoin's origin story is quite fascinating. It all goes back to 2008 when Satoshi Nakamoto published a whitepaper."

"A whitepaper, huh? Sounds official," Alice cut in.

"It was," Bob explained. "This whitepaper outlined a revolutionary concept: a peer-to-peer electronic cash system. Imagine being able to send and receive money directly, without relying on banks or other financial institutions."

"No banks involved? Like, *bank-less*?" Alice asked.

"Precisely," Bob affirmed, nodding. "Satoshi Nakamoto envisioned a giant global network where everyone can voluntarily participate and verify Bitcoin transactions. It was a bold idea, and it definitely challenged the status quo."

"And it worked?" Alice inquired.

"It certainly did," Bob replied without hesitation. "You know, While Satoshi's true identity is still a subject of much debate—some even convinced they know exactly who it is—we still don't have everyone on the same page about it. I've got this gut feeling that Satoshi must be a man and I'm just going to trust that instinct. Despite the mystery, his invention sparked a global movement, and Bitcoin, the cryptocurrency born from his whitepaper, became the trailblazer that remains the most well-known today."

"But Bob, why does it really matter to know who Satoshi Nakamoto is? There must be a reason why he wants to stay anonymous in the first place, right?" She asked.

Bob nodded. "I guess some people are just obsessed with figuring out the person, or team, behind something this groundbreaking. It's almost like an unsolved mystery people can't help but want to crack."

Alice tilted her head slightly, contemplating the mystery. "Honestly, if I were Satoshi, I probably wouldn't want anyone to find out who I am even now. I mean, wouldn't that just complicate things?"

Bob chuckled, nodding in agreement. "Exactly. If I were in Satoshi's shoes, I would probably want to keep my identity a secret too. It just makes things simpler. No drama, no pressure from the media or investors."

Alice leaned back, crossing her arms thoughtfully. "Right? Plus, it keeps the attention on Bitcoin itself rather than the person behind it. It allows the community to thrive without any one individual overshadowing the whole thing."

She continued, "I would also be worried about regulators poking their noses in. If people knew who I was, it could open the door to all sorts of scrutiny and pressure. Imagine being the face of something that challenges traditional finance—it would be a huge target for regulators who might not like the idea of a new currency shaking up their control."

As they sipped their drinks, Alice leaned in, her curiosity piqued. "You know, all this talk about anonymity makes me wonder: if someone were to suddenly claim to be Satoshi Nakamoto, how could we really know if he was telling the truth?"

Bob considered this for a moment. "The easiest way for someone to prove he is Satoshi Nakamoto would be to spend some of the Bitcoin that's believed to be his. If he could do that, it would add a ton of credibility to his claim."

Alice frowned slightly, "But what if Satoshi genuinely lost access to his Bitcoin? That could easily complicate things."

Bob nodded, acknowledging her point. "True, that's a possibility. But then again, if someone is claiming to be Satoshi, you would of course expect him to have a way to prove it, right? It's a tricky situation, for sure."

He continued, "That reminds me of that old story about the two mothers and the baby. You remember how the wise king figured out who the real mother was?"

Alice smiled, recalling the tale. "Oh, yes! The king suggested cutting the baby in half, and the false mother agreed, but the real mother immediately cried out, saying she would rather give him up than see him killed."

"Exactly!" Bob said, leaning forward with more energy. "In my opinion, if someone claims to be Satoshi but can't spend the original Bitcoin, it makes you question if they're telling the truth. I mean, not being able to spend it doesn't harm Bitcoin directly, but think about it—Satoshi staying anonymous was probably deliberate. If the real Satoshi were to suddenly show up now, it wouldn't necessarily be about taking control or changing how Bitcoin works. The real impact would be in the uncertainty it causes, especially on a psychological level. People would start asking: What does Satoshi want? Why now? And most importantly, what's the endgame? Even without technical control, Satoshi's presence could create this authority figure that people might feel compelled to follow—or resist. That kind of uncertainty, whether it's about Satoshi's motives or potential influence, could disrupt the community. In my view, the real Satoshi wouldn't do anything to harm Bitcoin—even if it meant staying anonymous and giving up any recognition, just like the real mom in the story who wouldn't let the baby get hurt."

Alice thought for a moment. "So you're saying anyone who truly cares about Bitcoin's future, like the real Satoshi— and assuming he is a good guy, would probably prefer to remain in the shadows?"

"Exactly," Bob nodded. "It's almost like a test of character."

Alice leaned forward, her brow furrowed in thought. "But what if the real Satoshi shows up, let's say not for fame or recognition, but because they think today's Bitcoin has strayed too far from the original vision? Like, what if they want to steer it back on course? Would that make a difference?" she asked.

Bob nodded thoughtfully, "Satoshi always pushed for Bitcoin to be this open-source, decentralized project, right? Give credit to the developers, let the community decide. But imagine if after all this time, this so-called 'real' Satoshi suddenly pops up and says, 'Nah, this isn't what I meant.' It would be kind of ridiculous, almost hypocritical, wouldn't it? Almost like a long con. I mean, he's been anonymous, preaching about avoiding a single point of trust—no governments, no banks—but then if he steps in and claims his vision is the only one that matters, he would basically be making himself the *exact* central authority he warned us about. That would feel like a massive bait-and-switch. It would be like the whole decentralization talk was just a smokescreen to put himself on a pedestal as the one 'trusted party' after all. Pretty ironic, huh?"

He shrugged and continued with a hint of amusement in his smile. "Honestly, I'm not that interested in finding out who he is. Bitcoin is what it is today, regardless of who created it. Even if the real Satoshi suddenly came forward and said, 'This isn't what I envisioned,' how would that change anything? He was there from the start, so why wait until now to voice concerns?"

Alice pondered this for a moment. "That's a fair point. The community has evolved, and Bitcoin has taken on a life of its own."

"Exactly," Bob continued. "The idea has grown beyond any one individual. People have built businesses, communities, and even entire ecosystems around it."

Alice nodded, her brow furrowing slightly. "So, you think it's better for the identity of Satoshi to remain a mystery?"

"Maybe," Bob replied. "There's a certain beauty in the anonymity. It keeps the focus on the technology and the community rather than on a single figure. And let's be honest, the allure of Satoshi's identity adds to the mythos of Bitcoin. It's part of what keeps people interested. But you know, Satoshi really didn't want us to keep treating him like this mysterious shadowy figure.[1] He wanted the spotlight to be on the technology and the community, not just him. And honestly, while that air of mystery makes Bitcoin a bit more captivating, it can kind of overshadow all the hard work the

---

[1] Gavin Andresen's last email exchange with Satoshi. Email subject: alert key. 26 Apr 2011, 10:29. Source: http://gavinandresen.ninja/eleven-years-ago-today

developers are doing. At the end of the day, it's the community that really keeps this whole thing going."

Then, suddenly Bob leaned in, curiosity shining in his eyes. "So, Alice, what do you think could be behind someone suddenly claiming to be Satoshi?"

Alice paused, mulling it over. "Well, they could either be the real Satoshi, or maybe they know Satoshi personally—like, touch wood," she said, tapping her knuckles lightly on the table, "if he has passed away or can't defend himself anymore."

Bob raised an eyebrow, intrigued. "That's an interesting angle. What makes you think that?"

Alice shrugged, her brow furrowed in thought. "Look, if someone were bold enough to step forward and make that claim, it might mean they either have the real proof or they're trying to fill a void left by someone who can't speak up. It's like they would want to stake a claim for a legacy that might be fading."

Bob grinned, shaking his head in amusement. "You know what? It makes even more sense if someone were to make that claim publicly and then we hear nothing from the real Satoshi. That's the real kicker. If the real Satoshi is out there, why choose to stay quiet?"

His grin turned darker, and he leaned in with a glint in his eye. "And let's not forget, everyone loves to paint this noble picture of Satoshi—the visionary, the genius who gifted the world Bitcoin and then disappeared like some kind of hero. But… what if he's not all that?" His voice dropped a little, taking on a more conspiratorial tone.

He continued, "I mean, think about it. We don't really know who he is. What if the real Satoshi isn't this selfless figure everyone imagines? What if—and hear me out—Satoshi's grand plan wasn't as benevolent as we all like to think? What if Bitcoin was just phase one of something bigger? Something… less innocent."

Alice raised an eyebrow, intrigued but cautious.

Bob lowered his voice, clearly enjoying the wildness of the idea. "Picture this: Satoshi pops back up, but not to guide Bitcoin or protect its legacy. What if he's been waiting for the right moment to completely destabilize it? Dump all those early Bitcoin he's holding, crashing the market, or even worse—what if he reveals some hidden flaw or backdoor in the system? Something he's had in his back pocket all along, ready to pull the rug out from under everyone?"

He leaned back, eyes gleaming. "Everyone's built this perfect image of him because he's gone. But what if he was never the hero of the story? What if he's the villain, waiting in the shadows, ready to blow the whole thing up when no one's expecting it? It's the perfect cover—disappear, let everyone do the work, and then come back and knock it all down."

He added, "Furthermore, let's not rule out the possibility that Satoshi's original intentions were pure, but as the price of Bitcoin skyrocketed, greed could have taken over. You wouldn't want people to know your identity if your plan is to dump your stash on them, right? It's like the perfect setup—stay hidden, let the hype grow, and then, when no one's expecting it, cash out. That would shake the trust in Bitcoin like nothing else."

Alice blinked, trying to process it. "That's... pretty dark, Bob."

He shrugged, still grinning. "Hey, it's just a thought. People like to assume the best because they love their myths. But in the end, we don't really know anything about him. And sometimes, the real twist is that the villain was hiding in plain sight all along."

Alice shuddered slightly, her expression serious. "That's a pretty scary thought, Bob. I wonder if it's almost time for Satoshi to show up, considering how high the price of Bitcoin is now."

Bob scratched his chin, his earlier grin fading a little. "I really don't know. I mean, I hope I'm just exaggerating things. It's fun to speculate, but, man, if something like that were true... it would be wild."

"Bob, considering all the speculation and the possibility that the real Satoshi could be someone with questionable motives—or even someone who's no longer around—it just makes me wonder why you still advocate for Bitcoin and crypto so passionately," she said, searching for insight into his mindset.

Bob shrugged, a playful grin spreading across his face. "Honestly? I only invest what I can afford to lose. That's my rule of thumb. I mean, I'm genuinely passionate about it, but let's be real—life loves to throw curveballs."

Alice chuckled, nodding in agreement. "Yeah, I get that. It's like a rollercoaster ride—you've got to buckle up and enjoy the ride, but don't go putting all your savings on it!"

Then, Bob chuckled, realizing he had veered off topic. "Ah, I got carried away talking about the whole mystery of Satoshi. Your question was about why would anyone be willing to pay a high price for Bitcoin, without even a government guaranteeing its value, right?"

He paused, gathering his thoughts. "Well, Bitcoin wasn't always this pricey. Back then, it was practically dirt cheap. A few bucks could get you a decent amount, if you even cared about it. Its rise to prominence was gradual at first, mostly attracting tech enthusiasts and those disillusioned with traditional banking systems. But the idea of a *bank-less* currency secured by some innovative methods definitely captured people's imaginations." He recounted, a sense of history in his voice.

"Don't leave me hanging, Bob. Spill the digital beans." Alice continued, polishing off the last crescent of her croissant in a single, decisive bite.

Bob responded. "Bitcoin's value is a real head-scratcher. Let's think of it like launching a new product. Imagine this revolutionary gadget, unlike anything people have seen before."

"At first," Bob continued, "there's a small group of tech enthusiasts who get super excited about it. They're the early adopters, tinkering with the product, figuring out its quirks. But most people?

They're skeptical. 'What do I need this weird thing for?' they think. Bitcoin was kind of like that in the early days. A small group of tech-savvy folks saw its potential, but the general public wasn't convinced. In fact, most people didn't even aware of its existence. Plus, there were bugs, security issues – kinks to iron out, just like any new product development."

"So, how did it go from there?" Alice asked.

"Here's where it gets interesting," Bob said. "The Bitcoin community started working on improvements, addressing the security issues. They also had to figure out how to actually use this new digital money. Back then, a notorious online marketplace called *Silk Road* emerged, which unfortunately used Bitcoin for some shady transactions."

Alice grimaced. "Not exactly the best marketing strategy."

Bob chuckled. "But it did get people start talking about Bitcoin, even if for the wrong reasons. Meanwhile, the core idea – a secure, peer to peer digital currency – started to resonate with some folks. They saw the potential for fast, anonymous transactions that can bypass the banks, even if it was for illicit activities."

"So, it was a combination of constant improvements, finding use cases, and some not-so-ideal publicity?" Alice summarized.

"Indeed," Bob agreed. "Slowly, more and more people started paying attention. News outlets picked up the story and investors got curious. Back in the early days, there was this exchange called Mt. Gox. Ring a bell?" He watched her face for a reaction, knowing this was why she had come to Tokyo.

Alice's eyes lit up. "Of course! That's part of why I'm here. Mt. Gox was the first big exchange, right?

" Yep," he nodded, pleased to see her curiosity spark.

He resumed. "Back then, Mt. Gox was *the* place to trade Bitcoin—it was practically the heartbeat of the whole scene. People could finally exchange Bitcoin for traditional currency, and it was like a dam breaking. Suddenly, Bitcoin wasn't just this quirky internet idea; it became a commodity people could buy, sell, and invest in."

Alice leaned forward. "So that's what really put Bitcoin on the map?"

Bob smiled. "Exactly. And the more people traded, the more valuable it became. The whole thing snowballed, but it wasn't without its chaos—Mt. Gox itself collapsed spectacularly later on. That part you probably know."

Alice nodded, a little somberly. "Yeah, I read about it. It must've shaken the community."

"Big time," Bob agreed. "But even with that setback, the impact Mt. Gox had on Bitcoin's visibility was undeniable. And the rise continued, despite all the bumps along the way. Bitcoin was no longer just an experiment—people believed in its potentials, invested in it, and watched its value climb as the demand grew."

She looked out the café window, as if seeing Tokyo differently now. "It's wild to think how something that began here could end up shaping things so much."

"Right?" he nodded. "The journey was messy, but every step—good or bad—has only deepened people's interest and commitment. And from there, well... the rest is history."

"So, the value essentially comes from its growing network and people's belief in its potential?" Alice mused.

"Well, Alice, here's how I see it: Bitcoin really feels like a *conviction* asset. It's this digital currency that was born out of a strong belief that it could be a real alternative to traditional money. It's like a wake-up call for the old financial system, pushing it to adapt or face the risk of becoming outdated."

Potentials

Alice's eyes widened in realization. "That's fascinating. But what potentials are we looking at here?"

"For example, Alice, its ability to solve real-world problems such as to provide greater financial inclusion, especially to those who are *unbanked* or have limited access to traditional financial services. Take El Salvador for instance. According to President Nayib Bukele, about 70% of people in the country don't have a bank account, which basically means they're 'unbanked.'[2] But they adopted Bitcoin as their official money, alongside the USD, which has been their official currency for years, hoping that Bitcoin can help improve the situation."

Alice's brow furrowed as she heard the term "unbanked." It struck a chord. "Unbanked... that reminds me of *Providian*, Bob" she said thoughtfully, recalling what she knew of the credit card company.

"I remember how they targeted financially vulnerable people, offering them credit cards and being accused of deceiving and unfairly charging their customers. I suppose it's different from what you're talking about, but in a way, it makes me wonder—could Bitcoin really help, or might it end up exploiting people in the same way?"

Bob leaned back in his chair, considering Alice's concern. "I see where you're coming from," he said thoughtfully. "But Bitcoin is different. Unlike traditional financial systems, Bitcoin isn't controlled by a single entity or organization. This means there's no central authority that can manipulate or take advantage of users."

---

[2] https://x.com/nayibbukele/status/1401341311853252613

Alice tilted her head slightly as she listened, weighing his words. "I get what you're saying," she responded, her voice still tinged with skepticism.

"But Bob, you mentioned that Bitcoin could help the unbanked in El Salvador. Wouldn't it be even more confusing and risky for them? Bitcoin is a whole new concept compared to cash or a bank account. If they're already struggling with the existing system, wouldn't introducing Bitcoin just make things more complex? It feels like they're trying to leapfrog an entire stage of financial development, jumping from limited access to banking straight into a new currency system that even developed countries are still trying to figure out."

"That's a valid concern," Bob acknowledged. "While the transition to using Bitcoin presents challenges due to its complexity, it appears that El Salvador sees it as an opportunity to address the limitations of its traditional banking system, reduce remittance costs, attract investment, and prepare for future technological advancements. But let's be clear, the average Salvadoran doesn't need to be a crypto expert. A user-friendly app handles the technicalities. It's about convenience and accessibility."

Alice leaned back, crossing her arms as she considered his words. "Bob, I've been thinking," she began, her eyes narrowing slightly, "to use Bitcoin, people need to buy it first. However, many of them don't even have a bank account. If they don't have a bank account, how can they buy Bitcoin since everything is digital? Don't you think there's something wrong with that?"

Bob smiled, raising a finger as if he had been waiting for this question. "Good question. What if there was a machine that could turn your cash into Bitcoin? Think about a cash deposit machine: you deposit your cash, and it becomes digital." he replied.

Alice's eyes widened. "You mean, like a Bitcoin ATM?"

"Exactly," Bob said, his face lighting up with enthusiasm. "A Bitcoin ATM that also functions as a cash deposit machine. This is simpler and cheaper than setting up traditional bank branches, especially in rural areas. Most importantly, it functions without a bank account."

Alice pondered this deeply and immediately came back with another argument. "But, Bob, if so many people don't have a bank account, doesn't that suggest they can live without banks? If that's the case, labelling the 'unbanked' as a problem isn't just misleading—it seems like the crypto community is creating a narrative to serve their own interests. It feels deceptive, as if they're inventing a problem to justify promoting Bitcoin. These people might be perfectly content using cash in their daily lives, so why push the idea that they need Bitcoin?"

"I see your point," Bob nodded. "That being said, it's easy to oversimplify the issue of the 'unbanked.' It is true that not everyone who doesn't have a bank account is actively seeking one. However, to say that some people aren't shut out from financial services overlooks the challenges many face, especially in developing countries. Consider this: in some countries, particularly, many women lack personal identification documents such as national ID cards, which are often required to open a bank account or conduct financial transactions. They often rely on their husbands or other male relatives to access bank accounts. This dependence can be risky—if the men in their lives are unavailable, untrustworthy, or abusive, women may lose access to their own money, leaving them financially vulnerable and unable to support themselves independently. And for many, poor credit history makes it impossible to even open a bank account. For people like that, traditional banking has clearly failed them. The bottom line is, it's not about forcing Bitcoin on anyone, but about providing an option. If people choose to continue using cash, that's their prerogative. But for those seeking alternatives or facing limitations with traditional banking, cryptocurrencies can offer a viable solution."

Bob continued, leaning in slightly to emphasize his point. "We should also understand that a significant portion of El Salvador's economy relies on money sent home by their citizens working abroad. Traditionally, these remittances have been sent through banks or money transfer services, which often come with hefty fees and delays. These delays can be caused by things like the limited working hours of banks, processing times, or even the difference in time zones between sender and recipient. Sometimes it takes several days for the money to get to the family back home. This isn't just inconvenient—it can be serious, especially if the family needs the funds urgently for things like medical emergencies or essential living expenses. With Bitcoin, transactions can be carried out 24/7, without the constraints of bank hours or processing delays. This means that money can be transferred quickly, at any time, which could make a significant difference in urgent situations. Of course, Bitcoin has its own complexities, but the ability to process transactions around the clock is a notable advantage."

Alice's eyes softened with slight understanding as she nodded. "But wouldn't they still need to exchange their dollars for Bitcoin first? And what about the volatility of Bitcoin? Wouldn't that be risky?" she asked. "Plus, wouldn't they face high conversion fees when converting their money to Bitcoin? It seems like no one really talks about those costs, which could make it more expensive than they think, and it could end up costing more than just using a traditional remittance service."

"That's a valid concern," Bob admitted, his expression becoming serious. "While Bitcoin's price can fluctuate, the potential for savings on remittance fees could outweigh the risks for many people. Additionally, if they expect Bitcoin's value to increase, they could see their remittance grow significantly. For example, if you convert $2,000 into Bitcoin at a rate of $40,000 per Bitcoin, you would get 0.05 BTC. If Bitcoin's price then rises to $60,000, that same 0.05 BTC would be worth $3,000."

Alice's eyes widened again in realization. "Oh, so they're not just saving on fees—they're also hoping the value of their money will increase?"

"Correct," Bob confirmed. "It's a way to potentially get more value out of their hard-earned money. And speaking of conversion fees, you're right, Alice, a lot of people don't consider the conversion fees when they talk about how cheap Bitcoin transfers are. It's true that transferring Bitcoin from one place to another can be cheaper than traditional remittance services. But the tricky part is converting traditional money into Bitcoin and back again. Those fees can significantly add up, and in some cases, they might even cancel out the savings you get from avoiding traditional remittance fees."

Bob paused, thinking for a moment. "Imagine if people could just get their salaries in Bitcoin. They wouldn't have to worry about converting their local currency into Bitcoin and could use it directly for their everyday purchases. In El Salvador, where Bitcoin is officially accepted as a form of money, people don't need to convert Bitcoin back into their local currency, which makes things a lot easier. But in most places, people still depend on their local currencies, and converting between the two can be a big hassle. It's an important thing to consider when talking about Bitcoin as a solution—there's still a lot of groundwork and adoption needed before it can be a practical choice for everyone."

Although Alice valued Bob's candid reply, a trace of skepticism still danced in her voice. "Sorry for all the questions, Bob. I'm just trying to wrap my head around this. I mean, isn't the real issue with the 'unbanked' more about El Salvador's own economic and financial infrastructure? Wouldn't fixing those be a more sustainable solution in the long run? Adopting Bitcoin without addressing fundamental issues seems like a desperate gamble to me, possibly even a way to deflect attention from domestic problem. Don't you think?"

Bob stroked his chin thoughtfully. "That's a sharp point, Alice. You're right, poverty, lack of funding, limited financial knowledge, unattractive banking products can all lead to a large population that either do not immediately need banking service or struggle to have access to banks. But here's another way to look at it: for El Salvador, trying to fix a broken traditional system might not be the best way forward."

"Okay, Bob, I'm all ears." Alice affirmed she was listening.

"Alice, consider if El Salvador remains entrenched in the traditional banking paradigm and doubles down on it. This would require significant investments in expanding physical bank branches, upgrading outdated infrastructure, and navigating complex regulatory and operational hurdles. By the time these improvements are implemented, the financial landscape could drastically change, leaving the country's banking system ill-equipped to compete in a digital-first world. Most importantly, they risk replicating the challenges faced by many developed nations, such as exorbitant operational costs, inability to innovate within the constraints of the legacy banking model, and a growing distrust from the public as the economy struggles despite endless excuses. A fresh approach could potentially circumvent these challenges altogether. By simultaneously harnessing the power of Bitcoin, El Salvador can explore new avenues for economic growth and development. Essentially, the country's adoption of Bitcoin represents a bold bet on the future."

Bob proceeded to offer some interesting personal perspectives on that matter. "Look, developed nations often carry the weight of established financial systems burdened by ingrained inefficiencies that real changes are incredibly difficult. And for a country like El Salvador, with such a large unbanked population, this might actually be an advantage. They don't have the same old systems holding them back. By adopting Bitcoin, they could jump right into a new form of financial system. It means they can innovate without being stuck in the past. They have the chance to build something new and potentially more inclusive and giving more autonomy back to the people. While there are definitely risks with Bitcoin, the potential benefits could outweigh them."

He paused to gauge her reaction. Alice nodded slowly, processing his words. "It makes sense. It's hard to change a system that's been around forever. I hadn't considered that perspective, Bob. It's a bold move, but it could pay off in the long run."

Bob leaned back in his chair, crossing his arms. "There's also a symbolic element to consider. By adopting Bitcoin, El Salvador is sending a message to the entire world – they're not content with the status quo and are actively seeking new solutions."

"Now, the results so far have been mixed. While some Salvadorans have embraced Bitcoin for remittances, there have been challenges. Volatility is a concern, and there's been a learning curve for many regarding using a new digital currency. Adoption hasn't been as widespread as the government might have hoped. It's still early days, though. El Salvador's experiment with Bitcoin is being closely watched by the world. Whether it proves to be a lifebuoy or a risky gamble remains to be seen." Bob shrugs.

"Bob, I must admit that's an interesting perspective. But somehow it appears that Bitcoin isn't really helpful in countries that have already achieved a high level of financial inclusion. What do you think?" Alice continued to press for more.

"You have raised another good point, Alice," Bob nodded. "In such countries, the immediate need for an alternative like Bitcoin might not be as apparent. That being said, take Lugano, a city in Switzerland, for example. They have allowed residents to pay taxes and other fees using Bitcoin.[3] This move isn't necessarily about financial inclusion. Bitcoin still offers several benefits even in such cases."

Alice's eyes sparkled with curiosity. "Like what?" she probed.

Bob replied. "Well, Alice, it is true that domestic bank transfers can be cheap – some places even do them for free. But for sending money overseas, they can be a total drag – slow and super expensive. Crypto can be way cheaper for international transfer because it cuts out the middleman – the banks. Remember how we talked about

---

[3] https://planb.lugano.ch

Bitcoin being a cheaper and faster way for Salvadorans to send money back home?"

He continued. "Traditionally, banks charge fees for currency exchange and processing international wires. Crypto transactions, on the other hand, happen directly between users on a peer-to-peer network, potentially reducing these fees significantly, although fees can still jump sometimes because of congestion on the crypto network, kind of like rush hour traffic."

"Hold on a second, Bob," she interrupted. "You are hinting the possibility of high fees even with cryptocurrencies. If that's the case, wouldn't that challenge the narrative of crypto being a cheaper alternative for money transfers?"

"Good catch, Alice. You're right, crypto transaction fees aren't always insignificant."

Alice was clearly not impressed. "So, are you now telling me these crypto people are sugarcoating everything? They paint this picture of a perfect type of digital money that allows cheaper overseas transactions, but are they all lies? Besides, even if sending money overseas through my bank is expensive, what's the big deal about crypto if it's not even that much cheaper?"

"There's some truth to that, Alice." Bob acknowledged with a patient smile. "Transaction fees can be all over the map, depending on the crypto you're using and how busy the network is at that moment. It's definitely not a one-size-fits-all solution."

Bob pulled out his phone, showing Alice something on the screen. "Let's say you're using… Ether, or, uh, 'eeth,'" he said, making the sound, as in 'teeth' but without the 't' sound.

Alice tilted her head slightly, repeating, "Eeth?"

He chuckled. "Yeah, 'eeth'—that's how most people say it. But actually, it's E-T-H, spelled out. People just shorten it to that." He smiled, then pointed at the phone. "It's the other big cryptocurrency next to Bitcoin, but everyday transactions can get pricey, especially when the network gets busy."

"See this graph here?" He tapped the screen, revealing a visual representation. "These are the current fees on its network. Notice the ups and downs? That volatility can translate to higher fees, especially when the network is buzzing with activity."

His voice now taking on a more explanatory tone, "So, sending a small amount of money might end up costing a significant portion just in fees. Imagine you want to send $10 worth of ETH to someone using a cryptocurrency. However, the fee for this transaction is $5. In this case, you're paying a fee that's 50% of the amount you're sending ($5 out of $10), which makes the transfer less cost-effective and defeats the purpose of using cryptocurrency for cheaper transfers. Having said that, there are some clever workarounds that can make things cheaper."

Alice raised an eyebrow, intrigued by this new angle. "Workarounds? How's that possible?"

"Imagine a highway with heavy traffic," Bob explained using an analogy. "Expensive transaction fees when the network is congested are like those expensive tolls during rush hour."

"So, these workarounds you mentioned create bypass lanes?" Alice asked, catching on.

"Close, but not quite," Bob reacted. "Instead of each transaction paying a hefty toll to use the main highway, they can bundle up together. Think of it like carpooling – everyone shares the cost, making it way cheaper for everyone involved."

"So, how cheap do these workarounds get, Bob?" Alice asked, curious about the practical implications of this "crypto-pooling" concept.

"Generally speaking," Bob clarified, "we're talking about going from potentially tens of dollars per transaction down to just a few cents or even fractions of a cent."

"Wow, that's a big difference!" Alice exclaimed. "So, potentially, crypto is made a more viable option even for everyday transactions then?"

"Exactly," Bob replied. "It's still evolving, but these solutions, called layer 2 protocols, are definitely a promising step towards cheaper and even faster crypto transactions. And speaking of speed, do you know that crypto transactions can be much faster, especially when dealing with different currencies and time zones?"

"Faster, huh?" Alice echoed. "How much faster are we talking about?"

"The speed of crypto transactions can vary depending on the specific network, but generally, they're much quicker than traditional bank transfers. Imagine sending money to your friend in Europe – with a bank, it could take a couple of days for the funds to clear, right?"

Alice nodded, recalling the sluggish pace of international bank transfers from her own experiences.

"With crypto," Bob continued, tapping his phone screen for emphasis, "that same transaction could be completed in a matter of minutes, sometimes even seconds. Again, it cuts out the middleman – banks and international clearinghouses – and allows for a peer-to-peer transfer directly between you and your friend."

Alice's eyes widened in surprise. "Wow, minutes instead of days? That is a significant difference. So, it's almost like sending an instant message, but with money?"

"Exactly!" Bob exclaimed, snapping his fingers. "That's the beauty of cryptocurrency for international transfers. Fast, secure, and potentially lower fees – that's the promise many see in this new technology. And the best part? It's available round the clock, so you can send or receive money at anytime, anywhere in the world."

Alice was not ready to give up yet. "So, Bob, this cryptocurrency thing definitely sounds interesting for sending money overseas," she responded. "But what about for everyday transactions within our own country? Aren't traditional methods like bank transfers or money-transfer apps fast and cheap? They're familiar to us, and it seems easier."

Bob nodded. "That's a good point, Alice. For domestic transactions, traditional money transfers reign supreme. They can be fast and free, especially between accounts at the same bank. Crypto probably wouldn't be your best bet in that situation."

"So, crypto's more for international transactions then?" she probed.

"That's certainly the gist of it," Bob replied. "However," he adds, holding up a hand, "I'm not saying crypto is better than domestic bank transfers for everyone."

Alice, confused. "Okay, but where are you going with this?"

"It's about choices, Alice," Bob explained. "While bank transfers are convenient for everyday transactions, there are situations where cryptocurrency is the preferred form of payment for some individuals. Simply put, sometimes people just prefer to use cryptocurrency instead of traditional money. And you can't send crypto through a traditional bank—at least, not yet."

"But Bob," Alice said, clearly not backing down, "using your own logic about choices, the reality is that most international businesses today still stick with traditional currencies like dollars or euros. Sure, crypto might be the way of the future, but right now it's not widely accepted for international payments. Almost all businesses are set up for traditional money, and that's what they expect. Just think about trying to buy supplies from a manufacturer overseas with crypto—they might not even know how to handle it! So, when it comes to actual transactions, especially across borders, traditional money isn't just a choice; it's pretty much a must-have for most businesses. Comparing crypto to regular money for international transfers isn't exactly comparing apples to apples, don't you think?"

Alice continued, her tone earnest as she elaborated on her point. "Plus, there are a lot of regulatory and technical issues with crypto that make it tough to use for everyday business transactions. Traditional money is regulated, stable, and just easier for most businesses to deal with."

"Okay, I'll admit," Bob said, raising his hand, "when I mentioned crypto being faster and cheaper, I might have been a bit one-sided. The truth is, international money transfers using traditional methods definitely have their own strengths. But what crypto offers is a unique option – a potentially faster and, in some cases, cheaper way to send money internationally."

Alice nodded, curious to see where Bob was going with this, as he clearly hadn't addressed the part about comparing apples to apples.

"Here's the thing," Bob continued. "when we compare crypto and traditional money, we're essentially comparing two different forms of the same concept – a medium of exchange. Think about it this way: we used to barter goods and services directly. Then came physical money, like coins and bills. Now, we have digital payment like bank transfers and, more recently, cryptocurrency. While they might be different forms of a similar concept, comparing them isn't necessarily comparing apples to oranges."

As Alice listened to Bob, her mind raced with reflections. It's true that bartering, physical money, and digital currencies all serve the fundamental purpose of facilitating exchanges. Bob makes a fair point about comparing different forms of the same concept. So, to make a fair comparison, she might need to set aside the factors that make traditional money seem better just because it's been around longer.

The advantages of traditional money, like its widespread acceptance and established infrastructure, are not inherent qualities of the money itself but are largely due to its long-standing presence and the systems built around it. These are external factors that don't necessarily reflect its intrinsic value or functionality as a medium of exchange.

In the same way, when we compare cryptocurrency, we probably should focus on its inherent features rather than just how it stacks up against the current, entrenched systems. It's about looking at what each system brings to the table in terms of their fundamental purpose and capabilities, without being overly influenced by the historical context or existing biases.

So, in essence, comparing crypto and traditional money directly actually makes sense if we focus on their core functions and potential, setting aside the external advantages that traditional money has gained through its established role.

Bob, seeing a flicker of understanding in Alice's eyes. "Look, I know this can be a lot to take in. Just remember, traditional money is a well-established form, while cryptocurrency is a newer, digital alternative. But both are tools for exchanging value. One might be more familiar, like a trusty hammer, while the other is a newer tool, like a power drill, with its own strengths for specific situations."

Alice, nodding slowly. "Okay, I think I'm starting to grasp it. It's about having the right tool for the right job, not necessarily replacing the old tools entirely."

"Precisely, Alice. Cryptocurrency adoption is certainly lower than traditional currencies right now. That's why comparing them might naturally seem like comparing apples and oranges. But what if we flipped the script?"

"Flipped the script? What do you mean?" Alice intrigued.

"Imagine a world where cryptocurrency adoption skyrockets. Let's say there's a 50/50 chance any business or individual would accept crypto. Now, factor in the potential for faster and cheaper transactions with crypto. In that scenario, wouldn't the convenience and cost savings make crypto a very attractive option?" Bob put forth a hypothetical scenario.

Alice, pondering the proposed scenario. "That's indeed a fascinating way to look at it, Bob."

Bob concluded with a satisfied nod. "It's really about having options and flexibility, Alice. However, it's also important to remember that these new options should address limitations of the existing methods, not just be different for the sake of being different."

A hush fell over the café for a moment as a young Japanese man at the counter fumbled with his phone, his transaction apparently taking longer than usual. Bob, ever observant, glanced at the café's payment terminal – a small device displaying a familiar orange QR code.

"Look over there, Alice," he whispered, gesturing towards the cashier. "See that guy paying for his drink?"

Alice followed his gaze, spotting the man. "Yeah, what about him?"

"He's actually paying with Bitcoin!" Bob's excited.

Alice raised an eyebrow, surprised. "Bitcoin? You mean that whole cryptocurrency thing?"

"The very same," Bob confirmed, leaning back in his chair. "It's fascinating how this technology is starting to be used in everyday situations."

"Wait, so how does that even work?" Alice leaned forward, her initial skepticism now giving way to genuine curiosity. "Isn't Bitcoin supposed to be super complicated to use?"

"It can be, but the core function is actually quite simple. Remember, Bitcoin is essentially a digital currency, like a virtual form of money," Bob said. "But again, like Ether, which we discussed earlier on, Bitcoin transactions can also be slow and expensive, which isn't ideal for everyday purchases like that coffee."

"There's a catch, again, huh?" Alice, unimpressed.

"The good news is," Bob said with a grin. "For Bitcoin, there is something called the *Lightning Network*. Think of it as a layer on top of Bitcoin, allowing for faster and cheaper transactions. It's like a separate channel where transactions happen almost instantly at a much lower cost."

He paused and emphasized, gesturing with his hands. "I want to make sure it's clear: the Lightning Network is *not* the main Bitcoin network. Instead, it's an extra layer built on top of it. The main Bitcoin network is where all transactions are recorded and verified securely. The Lightning Network works outside the main Bitcoin system, allowing people to send small payments faster and with lower fees. Only the final results of these transactions are reported back to the main Bitcoin network. So, the main network handles the overall security and record keeping, while the Lightning Network speeds up and reduces costs for everyday transactions."

Alice raised an eyebrow. "But isn't that defeating the whole purpose of Bitcoin? If we're using a different system for transactions, isn't it no longer the original Bitcoin?"

Bob leaned in, a grin spreading across his face. "That's a great question, Alice. The Lightning Network isn't a replacement for Bitcoin, but more like a smart detour. Think of it as a shortcut that still depends on the original Bitcoin network for security. Even though Lightning transactions happen outside the original network, they're still tied back to it. It's like cutting through the park instead of driving all the way around the city —you still end up at the same place, but you get there faster and with less effort."

Alice furrowed her brow, not entirely convinced. "I get what you're saying, Bob, but I'm not sure I agree. I mean, taking shortcuts might speed things up, but it feels like it could compromise what makes Bitcoin unique."

Bob tilted his head, thinking it over. "You've got a point there, Alice. Some people might feel like the Lightning Network is kind of drifting away from the heart of Bitcoin. I mean, it's definitely faster and cheaper, but it does make things a bit more complex. You know, it's like taking a shortcut that might make you a little lost if you're not familiar with the area. So, yeah, it's a trade-off, and not everyone's going to be okay with that."

Alice raised an eyebrow, quoting Satoshi's words. "And isn't Bitcoin supposed to be *electronic cash*? It's right there in the title of his whitepaper. Yet, look at Bitcoin nowadays—it's hardly usable as cash unless you go through something like that Lightning Network you talked about."

Bob exhaled deeply, thinking carefully. "The question then becomes: are people still supporting Satoshi's unprecedented vision, or are they celebrating what Bitcoin has evolved into today? Because those are two very different things. If you're still holding onto the idea that Bitcoin should be everyday cash, then honestly, you're probably frustrated with where it's ended up. But if you see Bitcoin more as *digital gold*—a store of value, something to hold onto as a hedge against inflation or government overreach—then maybe you're content with where it's at."

Bob leaned in, clarifying, "It's not like the 'gold' part was missing from the start. Bitcoin is Satoshi's 'electronic cash' *and* 'precious metal' all at once. If someone argues that Bitcoin doesn't work like electronic cash anymore and they come out saying they've got the 'original' version, well, they better be ready to honor both sides of it. You can't just strip away one part. It was always designed to be both—a way to move money and to store value like gold. That balance is key."

Alice leaned forward, curious. "So, what's your personal view on all this? Where do you stand on Satoshi's vision versus what Bitcoin has become?"

Bob took a moment, staring off as if he were organizing his thoughts. "Honestly, I don't really know," he said with a small shrug. "I'm not so much of a visionary. To me, Bitcoin is what it is today, whether we like it or not. It's not that Satoshi's vision is obsolete, but if you look around, there are other projects that have taken up the 'electronic cash' mantle—projects that seem to be succeeding where Bitcoin's original use case kind of stalled."

"But at the same time, maybe what we're seeing with Bitcoin isn't a failure of Satoshi's vision, but an 'adaptation.' I mean, Bitcoin's just like anything else—it has to adapt to what people actually want. It's not some strict rulebook that everyone has to follow without question. The whole idea is that it's *for* the community, and if the community is cool with using supporting systems that help Bitcoin work better as cash while it still acts as digital gold, then that's just it adapting to the market. People aren't here to follow some religious doctrine; they want something that works — they want solutions that fit their lives. And if that means adapting to stay useful, then so be it. Honestly, if Satoshi had known the 'gold' part would steal the spotlight from the 'electronic cash' idea, he might've pitched the whitepaper as 'Bitcoin: A Peer-to-Peer Electronic Gold and Cash System' instead. Sometimes, visions don't die, they just shift and expand into something no one expected."

Bob smirked, leaning back in his chair. "You know," he said, his tone more casual, "this is just how the world works. The louder one always wins. It doesn't really matter what Bitcoin was supposed to be—'electronic cash,' 'peer-to-peer money'—what people shout about now is 'digital gold,' and that's what sticks."

"In fact, it's not even about what's right or wrong anymore. It's just that the narrative people latch onto the hardest, the one that gets the most noise, that's what ends up shaping reality. Satoshi might've had one vision, but the louder voices spun it into something else, and that's where we are today. In the end, it's like everything else—the loudest story wins the day."

Bob leaned forward, a curious look in his eyes. "So, Alice, what do you think would happen if Satoshi suddenly came out and said, 'Hey, today's Bitcoin isn't what I envisioned'? Do you think the world would rally together to stop trading Bitcoin and stabilize the price to make Bitcoin more suitable to be used as a currency, or do you think they would just shrug it off?"

Alice thought for a moment, then shrugged. "I think most people won't be concerned. The reality is, Bitcoin has grown into something so much bigger than just Satoshi's original vision. It's like a living organism now, with its own momentum and community. People have their own stakes, their own beliefs, and I doubt they would suddenly drop everything just because Satoshi had a change of heart. At the end of the day, Bitcoin is bigger than any one person, even Satoshi. The market has a life of its own, and people aren't going to just obey a leader they don't even know anymore."

"And that's how cruel reality is," she added, her voice steady. "No matter how idealistic the vision might be, once something enters the world and people start to invest their hopes, dreams, and money into it, the original intent can easily get lost in the shuffle. It's almost like a child growing up and becoming their own person—Satoshi might be the creator, but Bitcoin has evolved beyond him. People will cling to what serves them best, regardless of where it came from or what it was meant to be. That's just how the game is played."

Bob sighed lightly. "I can't agree more. It's like a bittersweet reality check. And, like you said, it can be pretty brutal."

Alice's eyes darted toward that young man paying with Bitcoin, then back to Bob, as something clicked in her mind. "Hold on a second," she said, her gaze locking onto Bob's. "Speaking of Lightning Network, I thought the whole point was instant transactions. So why is he stuck waiting around?"

"Well, Alice, it's usually super-fast, but sometimes there can be delays. Maybe he needs a top-up, or the network might suffer congestion caused by malicious attack, or simply his internet connection is slow or unstable."

"Ugh, that sounds frustrating," Alice sighed, shaking her head as she watched the young man continue fiddling with his phone. "So much for instant coffee, huh? If this happens all the time, I don't see the point. Nobody wants to wait around forever for a payment to go through."

Bob nodded sympathetically. "These delays can definitely be a pain. But now that you see someone using Bitcoin right in front of your eyes, using cryptocurrencies to pay for our bills isn't necessarily a distant concept, agree?"

Alice tilted her head, pondering. "Interesting. It kind of reminds me of using mobile payment apps like Zapp or Apple Pay. They make everyday transactions much smoother compared to cash or swiping a card."

"These apps are certainly handy," Bob said, taking a sip of his coffee. "Think of them as digital wallets that let you access your existing bank account for payments. The actual transfer of funds might happen a little behind the scenes, but it still relies on the traditional banking system in the background."

"Right," Alice said, nodding. "So, the money isn't necessarily held within the app itself, it just gets authorized and transferred smoothly when I make a purchase."

Bob continued, "Now, the Lightning Network is clearly a whole different animal. It's a completely independent system, separate from traditional banks. It facilitates faster and cheaper transactions for Bitcoin specifically. Remember, Bitcoin itself operates on a different trust model. But here's the key takeaway: the Lightning Network isn't an app like Zapp or Apple Pay. It's more like the underlying infrastructure that enables faster payments, and there are actually apps built on top of it that you would use to make payments with Bitcoin."

"So, using Bitcoin like actual cash – for coffee, groceries – really relies on the Lightning Network? Without it, Bitcoin wouldn't be very practical for everyday purchases?" Alice questioned.

"Technically, you could still use Bitcoin for everyday transactions without the Lightning Network. But it would be somewhat slow, inconvenient, and expensive. Think of it like trying to buy groceries with a bag of gold bars – not exactly practical for a morning coffee run, right?"

Alice watched the young man finally disappear out the café door, his takeaway coffee cupped in one hand. A frown etched itself onto her face. Had he managed to use Bitcoin, or had the process proven too complicated, forcing him back to a more traditional payment method? Witnessing the attempt, happening right in front of her, sent a wave of unease washing over her.

The world, it seemed, was moving at breakneck speed towards Bitcoin and the whole cryptocurrency revolution. Here she was, just starting to wrap her head around the basics, while others were already putting it into practice. A pang of insecurity pricked at her. Was she already behind? How far behind, exactly?

Taking a deep breath, a flicker of determination ignited within her. No, she wouldn't let this feeling of being left behind paralyze her. The young man might have been a step ahead, but that didn't mean she couldn't catch up.

With renewed focus, a mischievous glint sparked in Alice's eyes. "Speaking of using it," she said, leaning closer, "Did you, by any chance, pay with Bitcoin today?"

Bob chuckled, "Nope," he admitted. "Cash, actually."

"But why not Bitcoin?" Alice pressed, tilting her head.

Bob smiled, "For me, Bitcoin's a great long-term capital gain investment, like gold or real estate investment," he explained. "I believe in its potential, and I'm holding mine for the future. Think of it like a fine wine – you wouldn't open a vintage bottle for every meal, would you?"

"So, it just sits there collecting dust… digitally?" Alice asked, a hint of sarcasm in her voice.

"Not exactly," Bob countered. "But I must admit, that's a really great point, Alice. The benefits of holding any cryptocurrencies, even Bitcoin, need to be tangible eventually. While I believe in its long-term potential, I also see the value in using it for everyday transactions, whenever possible."

Alice puzzled, "But wouldn't there be a dilemma when it comes to spending? What if you use it today and the price skyrockets tomorrow? You would miss out on those big gains."

"You're absolutely right, Alice. I guess that's the beauty and the curse of any investment, not just Bitcoin. There's always a chance you might miss out on future growth if you sell. You want to see your investment grow, but you also want to enjoy some of the benefits it offers at the present. It's a dilemma, for sure. I guess the key is finding the right balance between holding and spending," Bob replied.

"Maybe a little bit of both, then?" Alice suggested, a playful glint in her eyes. "Enjoy some of the digital coffee today, but keep some stashed away for the future gold mine?"

Bob laughed, "Exactly. It's all about finding what works for you. There's no one-size-fits-all answer when it comes to investing, especially in something as dynamic as Bitcoin. You just have to weigh the potential rewards against the opportunities you might miss and make the best decision you can with the information you have."

"And maybe not be too greedy, of course," Alice added with a wink. "After all, a little bit of digital coffee never hurt anyone, right?"

Bob chuckled once more, raising his empty cup in a mock toast. "To that, I can certainly agree."

Bob's phone buzzed insistently on the table. He glanced at the screen, a hint of apology in his eyes. "Excuse me, Alice, this looks urgent. Mind if I take this privately?"

"Of course, no worries at all," Alice replied with a smile.

She watched as Bob stepped away, taking the call outside. Left alone for a moment, she glanced down at her itinerary for the evening, a sudden realization dawning on her face.

"Oh dear," she muttered to herself. "Tonight's that delicious ramen place I wanted to try. They don't take cards, only cash. And I completely forgot…" Alice rummaged through her purse, the familiar clinking of coins confirming her fear. "Almost out of Yen!"

A beat of silence hung in the air as Bob returned, a relieved expression replacing his earlier concern. "All sorted out," he announced, taking his seat.

"That's good to hear," Alice said, forcing a smile. "Though, speaking of things needing to be sorted…" She hesitated, then plunged in. "Do you happen to know where around here I could exchange some US dollars for Yen? There's this incredible ramen place I have reservations for tonight, and they only take cash."

Bob chuckled, "Sounds like you need a quick Yen fix. Luckily, there's a currency exchange booth literally across the street. Won't take more than a few minutes."

Alice's eyes widened, "Across the street? Perfect! Thanks for the tip, Bob. Be right back!" She grabbed her purse and practically dashed out of the café, returning a few minutes later with a fresh wad of Yen.

Settled back down, Alice smoothed out her napkin with a satisfied sigh. "All set!" she declared, a triumphant grin on her face. "Delicious ramen, here I come!"

Bob smiled, "Sounds fantastic. Speaking of money exchange, though, did you know cryptocurrency can be used for more than just payments and hedging against inflation?"

Alice, now relaxed and ready to continue the chat, leaned forward in her chair. "How?"

"Well," Bob began, choosing his words carefully, "cryptocurrency isn't just a new way to pay for things anymore. It's also become a bit like a foreign exchange market, where people buy and sell different cryptocurrencies hoping their value will increase."

Alice's smile faltered slightly at the mention of "foreign exchange market." A hint of wariness crept into her voice as she asked, "Like forex trading? I dabbled in that a bit in college…"

Bob noticed the shift in her demeanor. "Did you enjoy it?"

Alice shook her head, a grimace forming on her lips. "Not exactly. It was all so… volatile. Felt like I was constantly chasing the next big trade, and it ended up being more stressful than exciting."

"Ah, I see," Bob said sympathetically. "Forex can be quite a beast, especially for beginners. The constant ups and downs can be nerve-wracking."

Alice nodded in agreement. "Exactly. Lost a bit of money too, which wasn't ideal on a college student budget."

"There you go," Bob said, leaning forward. "That's the key risk with any kind of trading, forex or crypto. You need to be comfortable with volatility and have a plan in place to manage your risk. But this volatility, while risky for those simply holding onto it, can be a source of income for active traders who understand the market and can make calculated moves."

"Still, it sounds like a wild ride," Alice mused. "Maybe not the best fit for me right now, considering my past forex rodeo."

"A wise assessment," Bob agreed." Cryptocurrency trading isn't for everyone. But for those willing to invest the time and effort to learn the ropes, it can be a lucrative option. However, the key takeaway is to be informed and understand the risks before diving in, regardless of whether it's forex or crypto."

"Absolutely," Alice said, nodding in agreement. "Thanks for opening my eyes to this other side of cryptocurrency, Bob. It's definitely something to keep in mind, even if it's not on my immediate to-do list."

"Of course," Bob replied with a smile. "And hey, at least your ramen adventure tonight won't be affected by the latest crypto crash, right?"

Alice laughed. "No doubt!"

Fallacy

Alice's skepticism wasn't quelled. "Alright, I get the lower fees and improved speed for overseas transfer is made possible by removing banks from the equation. But let's be honest, Bob, wouldn't that mostly benefit, well, people who don't exactly want a paper trail? You know, money launderers and whatnot?"

Bob, unsurprised by her challenge. "That's a common concern, Alice, and it's true that bypassing the banks can be a double-edged sword. But here's the thing – *blockchain* technology, the backbone of Bitcoin and most cryptocurrencies, is actually quite transparent. Every transaction on a blockchain is recorded publicly. While you might not see real names attached to the transactions, but the movement of funds is there for anyone to see. This is where it gets tricky. By analyzing these transactions, experts can track patterns and connections. Imagine you see money move from an account you recognize to another. Now you can start to guess who the real people behind those accounts might be."

He continued. "And here's the extra thing to consider: even if someone uses cryptocurrencies, they might still need to use a regular bank eventually. Think of it like wanting to use cash – you might want to exchange your crypto for regular money at some point. To do this, they would likely need to use a service that acts like a middleman, converting their crypto back to cash. These services often require real names and ID checks to comply with regulations, which can be a weak link in the anonymity chain. So, while complete anonymity is possible with complex methods, it's not easy. The more transactions you make, the bigger the trail you leave behind, making it easier for someone to potentially connect the dots and uncover the real identities involved. It goes without saying that large-scale transactions can easily attract more scrutiny and require even more sophisticated means to evade detection."

"Alright, alright," Alice conceded, a hint of defeat in her voice. "Maybe I've been a bit harsh on this whole crypto thing. Sure, the hidden identities part might attract some unsavory characters, but let's be honest, Bob, money laundering happens with regular banks too, right? Criminals always find a way, don't they? It's also like blaming the internet for cyberbullying." She winced slightly at the last word, a memory flickering behind her eyes.

Bob's smile softened with understanding. "Exactly, Alice. New technology can be misused, that's a fact of life. But the internet itself isn't inherently bad, just like cryptocurrency. Now, mind telling me more about this cyberbullying thingy? Sounds like you've had a rough experience?"

Alice hesitated for a moment, then continued, a flicker of frustration crossing her face. "It was just a few weeks ago, right after graduation. I posted some celebratory pictures on social media, you know, the usual stuff. And then the comments started – nasty, anonymous messages, making fun of everything from my outfit to my choice of major."

Bob's face hardened. "That's awful, Alice. Those trolls don't deserve a platform. I'm so sorry you had to go through that."

"It's okay," Alice said, forcing a smile. "The point is, just because something is anonymous doesn't mean it's good. And it doesn't make the technology itself bad, you know?"

"Absolutely," Bob agreed. "The internet itself isn't to blame for cyberbullying, just like cryptocurrency isn't inherently responsible for money laundering. It's all about how people choose to use these tools. In fact, law enforcement agencies are actually getting better at tracing crypto transactions thanks to the transparency of the blockchain."

He paused for a moment, letting the weight of his words settle. A thoughtful silence stretched between them for a moment. "Look," he resumed, his voice taking on a lighter tone, "those online bullies don't deserve to occupy any more space in your head. They don't get to define your experience with technology. How about we leave that negativity behind and dive deeper into this crypto business? I promise, it's a lot more fascinating than a bunch of keyboard warriors hiding behind usernames."

Alice, touched by Bob's kind sensitivity. "Alright, Bob," she conceded. "I am ready for more! Actually, this whole thing about cryptocurrency being an alternative and offers flexibility reminds me of how companies compete to offer the best smartphones. Features and prices are constantly changing, keeping things interesting for consumers."

Bob smiled. "Competition is a powerful force. Think about it – if there were only one company making smartphones, what kind of phones would we have? Probably pretty basic and expensive, right? Now, take traditional money, for example. For centuries, traditional forms of currency have been the dominant player. It's relatively reliable, everyone accepts it, but..." he trailed off with a shrug.

"But maybe a little stagnant?" Alice offered, picking up the thread.

"Exactly," Bob responded. "Competition, in this case, comes in the form of cryptocurrency. Suddenly, consumers have a choice. Maybe traditional financial institutions will need to step up their game to stay competitive. They might offer faster transaction speeds or lower fees to keep up."

"So, it pushes everyone to improve?" Alice questioned.

"Precisely," Bob responded. "Now, dominant players don't always welcome competition with open arms. Imagine a king who's ruled for years, suddenly facing a challenger for his throne. He might try to discredit the challenger, downplay the threat, or even try to change the rules altogether."

He continued. "I've heard some pretty wild theories that banks and financial institutions might be actively working to manipulate or suppress the price of gold. The rumor is that they could be dumping massive amounts of gold onto the market to drive its price down.

The idea behind this is that by keeping gold prices low, these powerful entities can safeguard the value of traditional currencies and maintain control over the financial system. They say gold, being seen as a hedge against inflation and a rival to conventional money, is a direct threat to their grip on the financial order. So, could it be that these institutions are playing a shadowy game to keep gold's value in check and protect their own interests? If that's happening with gold, it wouldn't surprise me if they tried similar tactics against cryptocurrency." Bob leaned back, spreading his hands in a shrug.

Alice chuckled. "Sounds a bit desperate, doesn't it?"

"It can be," Bob agreed. "But a healthy competition, even if it's initially met with opposition, can ultimately benefit everyone. Just like the king might be forced to become a better ruler in the face of a rebellion, competition in the financial world can lead to a more efficient and consumer-friendly system in the long run."

"So, it's not just about the technology itself, but the whole dynamic that gets set in motion?" Alice summarized.

"Absolutely," Bob confirmed. "Cryptocurrency might not dethrone traditional money entirely, but it forces existing system to evolve and adapt. It's a win-win situation, as long as both sides embrace the power of healthy competition."

Alice chimed in, "And it's ultimately about personal choice. Consumers can benefit from the competition by choosing the option that best suits their needs, whether it's traditional money or cryptocurrency."

"Indeed. Competition isn't about forcing everyone to adopt the new thing. Ultimately, a healthy market with diverse players benefits everyone – consumers with more control and better service, and established institutions with a push to innovate and stay relevant," Bob concurred.

Bob's words echoed in Alice's mind, replaying the multifaceted world of cryptocurrency.

It was digital money, yes, but it seemed different from the plastic she swiped, or the bills tucked in her wallet. A potential solution for the *unbanked* some said. Faster, cheaper overseas transactions – that was a win for everyday life. And then there was the investment side – a long-term play for potential capital gains or using this new volatile market to earn "daily bread."

Alice's inquisitive nature shone through as she started probing deeper, a nagging question surfaced. "I can see the appeal, Bob. But who decides its price?"

"You've hit the nail on the head," Bob paused for a moment and spoke. "The price of Bitcoin, and cryptocurrencies for that matter, is determined by a fascinating dance between what people are willing to pay for it and how many others want it – just like any other asset in a traditional market."

Alice nodded, a flicker of recognition in her eyes. "Right, so clearly it's not some fixed price set by someone?"

"No, it's not," Bob said, maintaining a neutral tone. "There's no single entity dictating the price. Instead, the market itself finds a sweet spot where buyers and sellers are happy to trade. Think of it like a bustling bazaar – the price constantly adjusts based on how many people are interested in buying Bitcoin compared to those willing to sell it."

"This process of figuring out the fair market value is called *price discovery*," Bob explained matter-of-factly. "It's a dynamic system that constantly reacts to various factors, including supply and demand, news events, and even the overall sentiment towards cryptocurrency's future."

"But how do all these people around the world agree on a price?" Alice pressed. "Can't someone just decide to inflate the value artificially?"

"There's certainly a risk of manipulation," Bob acknowledged, "But the key takeaway is that the price of cryptocurrency is constantly being determined by users around the world buying and selling on various exchanges. In fact, it's a complex system that involves not just human beings but trading bots, but that's also what makes it so fascinating."

Alice nodded, a thoughtful frown creasing her forehead. "But what if, hypothetically, for some reason, most people just stopped buying and selling crypto? Would the price just... freeze?"

Bob's smile faltered slightly. "That's an interesting question, Alice. The truth is, with no buying or selling activity, the price wouldn't necessarily freeze, but it would likely become very volatile."

"Volatile in what way?" Alice pressed, intrigued by this new scenario triggered by her own hypothesis.

"Imagine a market with few customers," Bob explained. "The value of the goods being offered becomes highly uncertain. Without fresh transactions, it could become difficult to establish a new price. The value could even plummet."

"So, it thrives on constant trading activities?" Alice pursued a clearer answer.

"Yes," Bob confirmed. "Without sufficient buying and selling activities, the price discovery process would essentially stall."

"Hmm, that's a bit of a risk then," Alice mused. "What if people lose faith in crypto altogether and just stop using it?"

"Actually, Alice, I genuinely don't believe people will lose faith in crypto entirely and just abandon it. We need to look at the deeper reasons why people are drawn to crypto in the first place."

"Deeper reasons?" Alice raised an eyebrow. "Like what?"

"It's a combination of psychology and societal trends," Bob explained. "Think about it. Cryptocurrencies tap into some fundamental human desires. The idea of financial autonomy, privacy, and having control over your own money without relying on banks is incredibly appealing. There's also a strong sense of community among crypto users, a feeling of being part of something revolutionary."

"Like a rebellion against the traditional financial system?" Alice chimed in.

"Exactly," Bob said. "There's a healthy dose of skepticism towards established institutions, a belief that crypto offers a more transparent and relatively fair system."

"But with all the ups and downs, wouldn't that scare people away?"

"It can be scary, especially for newcomers," Bob admitted. "There will definitely be some who lose faith, spooked by the volatility or disillusioned by the complexity. It's a natural part of any new technology. Remember the dot-com bubble burst? It didn't erase the power of the internet; it just reshaped it. That being said, there's also a powerful psychological factor called *FOMO* – the fear of missing out. When people see others making gains in crypto, it can be tempting to jump in, even with some risk involved. It's a double-edged sword."

"So, there will be some casualties, but crypto itself will survive?" Alice asked.

"I would think so," Bob affirmed. "The narrative surrounding crypto is too compelling to reject. And that narrative clearly resonates with a lot of people today."

He went on to say, "and we also need to consider that people have a sense of psychological commitment now towards crypto. They've invested time, money, and even emotions into this new technology. It's not something they'll easily give up on."

Alice, a spark of defiance lighting up her eyes, slammed her hand on the table (playfully, of course). "*Sunk cost fallacy*, Bob! Do you think it's possible that the entire crypto space has fallen victim to it?"

Bob gestured for her to elaborate, realizing that Alice had turned his previous argument on its head. He had previously argued that people wouldn't easily give up on crypto because they've invested so much in it, but now Alice was using that very point as a counterargument.

"Look at all the promises," Alice explained, her expression turning serious.

"A more transparent system, a power shift away from traditional institutions, and ultimately financial freedom. What if, crypto just doesn't deliver on those promises? What if people invested all this time and money chasing a vision that ultimately isn't achievable? Wouldn't that create a massive sense of disillusionment?" Alice put forth an intimidating case.

Bob acknowledged her concern and rephrased her argument for clarity. "I get your point, Alice. You are saying that people might get irrational and refuse to admit that crypto is not the solution they are looking for because they have invested heavily in it. For that very same reason, they might even consciously ignore or downplay new information or evidence that suggests the idea should be abandoned."

"Exactly, Bob. So wouldn't that just prolong the bubble if people keep pouring money in for fear of admitting failure and the associated stigma or personal disappointment?" Her voice carried a note of genuine curiosity, her eyes locked on his as she awaited his response.

Bob responded, "The *sunk cost fallacy* is a real concern for any investment, not just cryptocurrency. That being said, I believe some crypto projects have indeed fallen victim to it. Here's the thing, though: crypto is young, and, of course, it has had its share of bumps in the road. But none of those, in my opinion, pose an existential threat—except maybe for the constant pressure from regulators."

"Existential threat? Bob, that might be a bit dramatic, don't you think?"

Bob chuckled, "Maybe a bit, but regulations can definitely slow things down. Now, about your concerns. Transparency? Blockchain's core is built on it, so that's not going anywhere. A complete overthrow of traditional finance? Probably not. But crypto has definitely gotten their attention, motivating them to adapt and become more competitive."

He continued, "Next, financial freedom. That's a trickier one. I must admit that while cryptocurrencies themselves haven't explicitly promised financial freedom, the broader narrative around crypto often implies or suggests it. Crypto might not be a guaranteed path to riches, but it does offer a greater degree of personal control and autonomy of our money, including new ways for people to manage their money and potentially earn passive income. Look, my point is, crypto is already delivering on some of those initial promises. To me, the *sunk cost fallacy* argument doesn't quite fit here. In fact, crypto's potential is just starting to unfold. I do believe crypto is on the right track to deliver long-term value. Moreover, I feel we're all looking at crypto with tunnel vision, like, either it's going to be this world-changing, decentralized utopia, or it's going to crash and burn. But what if we're missing something in the middle?"

He paused and continued. "Remember the microwave oven? Initially created for radar, right? Not for heating up leftovers. It was a complete shift in purpose. Maybe crypto is on a similar path. It might not become the global currency everyone once dreamed of, but it could evolve into something equally significant. Perhaps it will revolutionize specific sectors, like supply chain management or micropayments. Or maybe it will become a crucial tool for emerging markets without established financial systems."

Alice jumped in, "But Bob, let's be honest, most people aren't interested in how crypto can improve businesses or industries. They just want to know how it can put money in their pockets. If it can't deliver on that promise in a substantial way, won't it lose much of its appeal?"

Bob nodded, a thoughtful look on his face as he considered Alice's point. He placed his hands on his knees and looked down for a moment, as if weighing his response carefully. After a brief pause, he met her eyes with a look of acknowledgment and insight.

"You're right, Alice. A lot of people are drawn to crypto because they see it as a way to make money, and if it doesn't deliver on that, it could definitely lose some of its appeal. But here's the thing: the same could be said for any investment. Even with stocks, nothing's ever guaranteed. Stocks can go up or down based on a ton of factors, and no one can predict the market perfectly. Still, people stick with stocks because they believe in their potential for long-term growth and returns. Most people don't buy stocks because they're fascinated by how a company operates or how it might innovate. They buy because they believe in the potential for returns."

He paused and resumed, "And just like with stocks, the long-term value of crypto isn't only about short-term gains. It's about what it could become. Sure, if it doesn't put money in people's pockets right away, some might lose interest. But those who see the bigger picture—the potential for crypto to reshape how we do business, transfer value, and create new opportunities—they're the ones who will stick around. And that's where the real growth happens. It's not just about instant profits; it's also about the broader potential and how it might change things down the line. Even if it doesn't hit all the marks right away, its underlying technology and the possibilities it brings keep people interested. Just like with stocks, it's not always about what's happening now but what might happen in the future. The key, I think, is to shift our focus. It's less about getting rich quick and more about building wealth."

Alice pondered, trying to wrap her mind around Bob's explanations. As she thought it over, she realized he had a point. So many people have lost money in the stock market, yet it hasn't disappeared. The belief in long-term value is what keeps investors around. Sure, some people might give up, but many others stay because they see the potential for growth in the future.

Bob watched as Alice seemed lost in thought. He recalled how this conversation had started with Alice's skepticism about cryptocurrency's potential benefits for the community, rooted in her concern about the *sunk cost fallacy*.

He took a deep breath, giving her ample time to process everything, gauging her reaction before adding, "And when I mentioned psychological commitment earlier on, I wasn't just referring to individual investors. The entire crypto ecosystem has invested heavily in time, money, and emotional capital. This creates a certain inertia, making it resistant to sudden shifts or setbacks. Even with market volatility and regulatory hurdles, the industry has a strong drive to persevere. The crypto world is pretty stubborn. So, it's not going to go down without a fight."

Bob leaned back, a grin spreading across his face as he lightened the mood. "Who knows, Alice? Maybe one day, when we've successfully colonized Mars, Bitcoin—or even something like *Dogecoin*—could become the first official currency up there. Imagine a Martian economy running on crypto, no middlemen, no borders, just decentralized digital money. It sounds funny now, but given how fast things are evolving, it's not that far-fetched!" He chuckled, clearly enjoying the thought.

Alice raised an eyebrow, smirking at the idea. "Martians trading in *Dogecoin*? That's a wild thought, Bob," she said, amused. "But hey, if we're dreaming about life on Mars, I guess anything's possible. Who knows, maybe crypto really will be the universal currency of the future—on Earth *and* Mars."

Her eyes scanning Bob's face. A flicker of determination, almost stubbornness, caught her attention. It was at that moment she realized that this wasn't just about technology or finance for Bob; it was about something deeper. Crypto is likely more than just a passing trend, she thought.

A thoughtful silence descended between them. The conversation had taken a turn, and Alice felt a growing sense of cautious optimism. Crypto's future might not be the utopian vision some held, but it could still be bright, as long as it stayed grounded in reality.

Part Two

A sliver of sunlight, finally breaking through the dense Tokyo afternoon, sliced across their table, casting a warm glow over Alice's nearly empty matcha latte cup. Her initial apprehension, now replaced by a spark of intense curiosity, took one last thoughtful sip, finding the frothy sweetness a welcome contrast to the complexity of the topic. The conversation had flown easily between them, with the hum of the café providing a comforting backdrop to their exploration of the brave new world of cryptocurrency.

"Wow," she said, setting down her cup with a soft clink. "That was a lot to take in, Bob. I never realized there was so much more to Bitcoin and cryptocurrencies than just being a risky online thing."

Bob was clearly pleased to see her growing interest. "It can be overwhelming at first, but it's definitely a fascinating concept. There's still a lot to learn, but you're definitely on the right track." He glanced at Alice's cup, now empty. "Actually, how about we refresh our drinks? Another matcha latte, or are you feeling adventurous?"

Alice raised her eyebrow playfully. "Adventurous? Hit me with your best shot, Bob. Maybe something a bit stronger? This crypto talk has my brain working overtime."

Bob smiled. "Great choice! The barista here makes a fantastic, iced Americano. I'll grab another round." He gathered his laptop and gestured towards the counter.

As Bob headed to the counter, Alice leaned back in her chair, her gaze drifting out the café window. She watched people bustling by on the street, absorbed in their daily routines. Absentmindedly tapping her fingers on the table, she jotted down notes on a napkin, reviewing key points from their earlier conversation about cryptocurrency.

Minutes passed, marked by the rhythmic clatter of the espresso machine and the soft murmur of other patrons. Finally, Bob returned with two iced Americanos, breaking her concentration.

"Here you go, Alice," he announced, setting down the drinks with a grin.

Alice smiled back, grateful for the interruption, folding the napkin, placing it beside her drink, and took a thoughtful sip of the iced Americano, savoring its cool bitterness before setting it down with a satisfied nod.

"Ah, refreshing," she remarked, before turning her gaze back to Bob. "Bob, my background's in finance, so I'm not exactly a tech whiz, but I'm not less curious about how the technical aspects of cryptocurrencies work."

Technology

Bob, taking a moment to savor his new iced Americano, leaned back in his chair. "This can be a bit of a mouthful, so let's break it down step-by-step. Think of Bitcoin as the granddaddy of crypto. It was the first to show everyone how to do secure money stuff without needing a centralized authority like a bank. Now, imagine a bunch of smart people took that idea and started experimenting. They created new kinds of crypto, adding extra features and trying new things. It's like Bitcoin had a bunch of really cool cousins."

Alice nodded slowly, the analogy sparking a flicker of understanding. "So, Bitcoin's kind of like the original recipe, and many newer cryptocurrencies are variations that add more ingredients and flavors?"

"Exactly. Now, imagine Bitcoin as a fancy new gadget," Bob said with a smile. "Like any innovative product, it has some unique features."

He held up one finger. "First, there's something called *cryptography*. One of the things it does is to ensure that Bitcoin transactions are authorized by the rightful owner through valid digital signatures."

He held up another finger. "Second, Bitcoin transactions get verified, processed, and bundled into blocks of data. Once a block is validated, it gets added to the chain of previous blocks in chronological order. There's only one recognized Bitcoin chain—the longest one—which the majority of the network agrees on as the 'official' record. That's where the name *blockchain* comes from. It's literally a growing chain of data blocks, all linked together."

He tapped the table for emphasis. "And here's the cool part – Bitcoin network doesn't rely on a single computer or a few coordinated servers to keep track of everything. Instead, it's spread out across a huge network of computers all over the world. These computers, called *nodes*, each have a full or partial piece of the blockchain. They constantly check with each other to make sure everyone has the same information. It's like having a million people watching every Bitcoin transaction, making it almost impossible for anyone to cheat or change the rules. If someone tried to mess with the record, the other computers would catch it right away and reject it."

"That's what *decentralization* is all about—no central server or trusted third parties, just like Satoshi envisioned.[4] Instead of depending on one authority, like a bank, to handle everything, the job gets spread across a whole network of independent computers. They work together to verify and record transactions on the blockchain, so no one has to put their trust in just one place. The system takes care of it by design. Interestingly, these days, that term—decentralization—has come to mean a lot more for the crypto community. It's not just about removing the middleman anymore; it's almost like a catch-all for everything that makes crypto different from traditional finance. Whether it's the transparency, the peer-to-peer setup, or how power gets spread around, decentralization has become this key idea that defines what makes crypto unique."

Bob leaned back, taking a breath. "So, to put it all together, imagine a giant public record that everyone can see, but no one can easily change. Transactions can only be initiated with a valid digital signature, stored in time-sequentially linked data blocks, and freely accessible to anyone across a global network of computers, with no restrictions or barriers to access. And the entire network has no central authority that tells people what to do and what not to do."

"Oh, and there's one more thing I should tell you before I forget. Unlike traditional currencies that can be printed indefinitely by governments, Bitcoin has a fixed supply. There will only ever be 21

---

[4] Satoshi's email to Wei Dai. Subject: Re: Citation of your b-money page. Sent January 10, 2009.

million Bitcoins in existence. This supply limit is a key aspect of Bitcoin's scarcity."

Alice pondered this for a moment. "But 21 million doesn't sound like a small number. Why is it considered scarce?"

Bob chuckled, not in condescension but in recognition of the million-dollar question that many pondered. "That's a common misconception, Alice. While 21 million might seem large at first glance, it's important to consider the global scale. With a growing population and increasing adoption of Bitcoin, each Bitcoin becomes more valuable as demand outstrips supply. This scarcity is what drives its potential as a store of value. Think of it like a collection of rare diamonds. There might be a few millions in existence, but that doesn't make them any less valuable, especially as demand for them increases."

"So, it's more about the fixed limit and increasing demand over time that makes Bitcoin scarce?" Alice questioned, a lightbulb seeming to go off above her head.

"Exactly," Bob said, snapping his fingers. "The scarcity of Bitcoin is a fundamental feature designed to ensure its long-term value and prevent inflationary pressures, like the kind you see with traditional currencies that are constantly being printed."

"That makes sense. It's like having a limited edition of something valuable that becomes more valuable as more people want it," Alice remarked, her voice conveying agreement.

Alice, intrigued by this new perspective on scarcity, reached for another bite of her croissant. Suddenly, a mischievous glint sparked in her eyes. She held the flaky pastry up, its golden layers catching the light of the café.

"Scarcity, huh?" she said, a playful smile dancing on her lips. "So, if there are only so many of these delicious croissants left, and everyone wants one, the more valuable each one becomes then." With a wink, she took another bite, leaving just a tiny crescent moon-shaped piece remaining.

Bob chuckled, readily following her lead, and savored the last bite of his own croissant.

"I'm simplifying a lot here," he said, "but hopefully, this helps you get a clearer picture of how it works. And keep in mind, we're just scratching the surface with Bitcoin—there are many other cryptocurrencies out there, each with its own unique features and approaches."

A look of realization dawned on Alice's face, pieces of the puzzle clicking into place. "So, this blockchain thingy…it's a giant, secure, and transparent public record. And since cryptocurrencies are digital monies, these public records are like…" She paused dramatically, raising an eyebrow at Bob.

Bob chuckled, a hint of amusement dancing in his eyes. "Like what, Alice?"

Alice leaned forward, a playful glint in her eyes. "*Public ledgers*, duh! You know, those big books accountants use to track everything?"

Bob threw his head back and laughed, a warm, genuine sound that filled the café. "Aha! So, the finance major finally surfaces! I was starting to think you were lost in the tech jargon jungle."

Alice's grin faltered slightly, a touch of embarrassment creeping in. "Okay, maybe a little," she admitted with a playful nudge. "But hey, at least I got the whole public record thing down, right?"

"But seriously, Alice, that's the key. Think of a traditional accounting ledger, a big book that tracks income and expenses. Now imagine a giant, digital version of that, accessible to everyone – that's the core idea behind not just Bitcoin but many other cryptocurrencies. Though, it's important to note that not all blockchains are public. Some are private, used by businesses to track things like supply chains or internal transactions."

Alice's playful expression faltered slightly. "Wait, private blockchains? So, not everyone can see everything?"

Bob leaned back in his chair. "Some companies or organizations might use blockchain technology for internal purposes, like tracking inventory or managing supply chains. In those cases, they wouldn't necessarily want a public record of all their transactions."

"Huh, that's interesting," Alice mused, her curiosity piqued. "So, public blockchains are for like Bitcoin and stuff, but private ones are more like... secret ledgers?"

Bob chuckled again, enjoying Alice's playful curiosity. "Not exactly 'secret'," he clarified, "but more like *permissioned*. Public blockchains, like the one Bitcoin uses, are completely transparent – anyone can see every transaction. Private blockchains, on the other hand, are more like permissioned ledgers. Only authorized users can access and see the information. Think of it like a company's internal financial records, secure and controlled, but still leveraging the benefits of blockchain technology."

Alice's mind raced as she absorbed everything Bob had said. But just as the conversation seemed to wind down, her thoughtful expression shifted, as if something had suddenly clicked. A look of realization crossed her face. Bob's explanation of the blockchain as a digital document that records cryptocurrency transactions was clear, but something about it still didn't quite sit right with her.

"Wait a minute, Bob," she said, her voice tinged with confusion. "So, Bitcoin's blockchain records Bitcoin transactions. But where's the actual Bitcoin—the *coin* itself? I mean, I get that the blockchain is digital, but where does Bitcoin physically exist? It sounds like there's no tangible asset, just records and entries."

Bob leaned in a little, making sure to keep things simple. "Well, Alice, Satoshi actually defines the Bitcoin's 'coin' as *a chain of digital signatures*.[5] When we talk about a coin being a chain of digital signatures, imagine this: A Bitcoin 'coin' isn't something physical, like a dollar or a coin in your pocket. Instead, think of it as a

---

[5] Bitcoin: A Peer-to-Peer Electronic Cash System. Section 2: Transactions. Satoshi Nakamoto.

receipt—a digital record that tracks all the people who have owned it before you. Every time someone sends Bitcoin, they add their 'name' —not their real name though, but rather their unique digital signature, to this record. The 'coin' is really just this receipt, showing the entire history of that Bitcoin from the very first time it was created, all the way to now."

Alice tilted her head, her eyes narrowing slightly. "I mean, I hear you, but I'm still not sure I fully get it. A Bitcoin 'coin' is just signatures? It's kind of confusing. So, when I send Bitcoin, does it get moved from my wallet to theirs, as if it's actually being transferred between the two wallets?"

Bob could see that Alice was still caught up in the idea of Bitcoin as an actual "coin," so he leaned in again, determined to help her see it differently.

"Alice, I think where it gets tricky is when you think of Bitcoin as an actual coin, like something physical or even a digital version of it. But Bitcoin isn't really a 'thing' you can hold. It's more like a record of transactions. What you're dealing with is more like the history of how a specific amount of Bitcoin has been passed from one person to another."

He paused, letting the words settle in. "Think of it like this: The Bitcoin blockchain is the digital ledger where all transactions are recorded. Rather than each Bitcoin's coin being an individual coin that moves from one wallet to another, it's more like the transaction itself that leaves a trail in this ledger. Every time Bitcoin is transferred, that transaction gets recorded on the blockchain. The ownership changes, but there's no 'coin' physically—or digitally—moving. It's just a new entry in the blockchain showing that now you own this part of the ledger, and someone else used to."

He watched her reaction, hoping this simpler version was starting to click for her. "Once you stop thinking of it like a coin and start seeing it as a record of who owns what, it starts to make more sense. It's really all about those transactions, not the idea of a 'coin' as we traditionally know it."

Alice was clearly struggling to process what he had just explained. He watched as her eyes flickered between him and the table, as though searching for something tangible to grasp onto.

"You're still not quite there, are you?" Bob asked gently, leaning forward. Alice glanced up at him, a bit sheepish, and shrugged.

"I get the idea, but it's hard to wrap my head around a 'coin' that doesn't actually move." She paused. "It's just... entries?"

Bob smiled reassuringly. "Yeah, it's a lot to take in. Let me try again. Think about how mobile payment apps work. When you pay with your phone, there's no physical cash involved. What you're really doing is moving around digital records and entries. It's all happening in a digital space, not with actual money changing hands."

Alice nodded slowly, following the analogy. Bob continued, "Consider how banks work with your money. When you deposit cash, it's not all stored in the bank physically. Instead, your account balance is a digital record of how much you have. Banks only keep a fraction of deposits on hand and lend out the rest. The money you see in your account is largely digital, a record of your balance, not the physical cash itself, even though you might think of it as physical cash."

He went on, "Credit operates in a similar way. When you borrow money or use a credit card, you're not receiving or spending physical cash. Instead, you're getting access to digital records. The credit system tracks how much you owe and borrow through these records. In fact, banks can create credit out of thin air. When a bank approves a personal loan, it doesn't hand over actual cash. Instead, it adds a digital entry to your account. No physical money changes hands; it's just a new digital record showing the loan. Of course, you can still convert that digital balance into physical cash if you want."

"That being said, the actual physical cash rarely comes into play. When you withdraw cash, it's only a small part of the money circulating in the system. The rest is being 'moved' digitally—transactions, payments, and loans are all managed through digital entries that don't involve physical money. In fact, most of the money that exists in the world today isn't in the form of cash at all. It's just numbers shifting between accounts."

Bob, now seeing a chance to tie it all together. "And that's pretty much how Bitcoin works too—it's all digital. There's no actual 'coin' moving around, just records of ownership changing hands. It's like credit or money in your bank account, except there's no bank in the middle managing it."

Alice nodded slowly but still looked uncertain. Bob could see that Alice's puzzled expression hadn't changed, even after his latest explanation. She tapped her fingers on the table, her eyes darting between him and her notes. It was clear that something wasn't clicking.

He gave a small smile and leaned back in his chair. "You know, Alice," Bob chuckled softly, sensing that they were going in circles. "Maybe I'm overcomplicating things here. Honestly, there's no harm in just thinking of these Bitcoin 'coins' as 'actual' coins in the digital world for now. Let the apps and those crypto-related websites handle the technical side of things—like the blockchain, signatures, all that stuff. For most people, all you need to know is that you have 'coins' and you can spend them. The tech works behind the scenes to make sure everything stays secure. So don't stress too much about the details right now. Just think of them as digital coins, and you'll be fine," he said.

Alice smiled, clearly relieved. "Thanks, Bob. I think I really needed to hear that." She leaned back, feeling the tension ease from her mind. "It's kind of refreshing to not have to dig into all the technical stuff. I just want to understand enough to use it without getting lost in the weeds. Sometimes it's nice to let the experts handle the complicated parts and just trust that it works."

Alice sat quietly, the hum of the café around her fading into the background as she mulled over Bob's explanation. The digital screen of her phone was aglow with the remnants of their conversation, but her thoughts were now miles away.

While she hadn't fully wrapped her head around everything yet, she was starting to get a feel for the basics. She had always pictured Bitcoin as a series of shimmering, coin-like images floating around in the digital ether, almost as if they were tiny virtual tokens moving from one place to another. But Bob had just shattered that mental image. Now, she realized that Bitcoin wasn't a physical object, even in the digital sense.

Alice stared pensively at her coffee before looking up at Bob with a thoughtful expression. "You know, Bob," she began, her brow furrowing as she spoke, "I used to imagine Bitcoin as these little digital coins, like shining tokens floating around in the digital space. I thought of them almost like virtual currency that you could see and move around. But now I see it's more about record-keeping and such. I'm starting to get that, but I'm still a bit unclear. Can you use Bitcoin for tiny payments, or is there a limit?"

Bob smiled, seeing Alice's continued curiosity. "Great question, Alice. You see, since Bitcoin is essentially just a record of transactions, these records can easily represent any fraction of a Bitcoin. This is why you can deal in tiny amounts. It's this digital nature that makes handling small transactions so easy. So yes, you can make tiny payments and handle tiny amounts within this system."

Alice leaned in, clearly intrigued. "Is there ever a point where you have to use a minimum amount for transactions? Like, is there a smallest unit of Bitcoin that you can't break down any further, or can you always use just a tiny bit of it?"

Bob smiled, sensing she was starting to make a connection. "Actually, Bitcoin can be divided into very tiny units, but you're right—there's a practical limit."

Alice glanced at him, her expression unsurprised, as if confirming something she had already been thinking about. "I figured there had to be. Just like with regular money, you can't break it down infinitely. There's always a smallest unit, like a penny or a cent."

"Exactly," Bob said. "For Bitcoin, that smallest unit is called a *satoshi*, clearly named after the creator of Bitcoin. One Bitcoin can be divided into 100 million *satoshis*. So even though Bitcoin can feel huge in value, you can spend or use just a fraction of it in a way that still works for small transactions. And just like you can buy a few slices of a pizza instead of the whole pie, you can buy a specific number of satoshis to invest a small amount in Bitcoin."

Alice's eyebrows lifted slightly. "A *satoshi*, huh? So you're telling me Bitcoin's equivalent to pocket change exists on that tiny level?"

"Yup," Bob replied. "And because Bitcoin is digital, those tiny fractions are recorded and tracked just like the larger amounts. It's what makes the system work for everything from large payments to microtransactions."

He paused for a moment, gauging Alice's understanding before continuing. "But here's where it gets a bit more complicated. Even though Bitcoin can be divided into such small units, the way Bitcoin transactions are processed and how fees work introduces some practical limits. Every time you send Bitcoin, the network needs to record that transaction on the blockchain. And for that, there's a somewhat 'voluntary' but 'necessary' fee. This fee isn't based on the amount of Bitcoin you're sending but on the size of the transaction data itself—the number of bytes being added to the blockchain."

Bob leaned forward, pulling out his phone to check the current Bitcoin price. "Right now, Bitcoin is priced at around $60,000. Let's say you want to send a tiny amount—like 1000 *satoshis*, which is 0.00001 Bitcoin. That amounts to just $0.60. Technically, you can send such a small amount, but here's the issue." He glanced back at his phone to confirm the most recent average transaction fee, wanting to provide an accurate figure. "The network still needs to use resources to verify and include your transaction on the blockchain, and based on the latest data, you could end up paying something like $0.70 for that transaction."

He paused to let the numbers sink in, then added, "So, the transaction fee could easily be much higher than the value of what you're sending. It's like paying a delivery fee that's more than the item itself—making it impractical for small transactions."

Alice raised an eyebrow, shaking her head slightly. "That sounds pretty ridiculous," she said, leaning back in her chair. "Why would I bother using Bitcoin if I'm paying more in fees than the amount I'm sending? It's like paying a $5 delivery fee for a $3 coffee. I might as well just use regular money—it seems way more practical for small transactions."

Bob nodded, sensing her frustration. "You're not wrong. Even people who use it all the time would likely agree. That's exactly why things like the Lightning Network exist. It's designed to handle smaller transactions more efficiently, without the same fee problem you would face using the *main* Bitcoin blockchain. Remember, the *main* Bitcoin network and the Lightning Network are two different things. The *main* Bitcoin network is what we usually talk about—the one where transactions are recorded on the blockchain. But the Lightning Network is a separate layer built on top of it. It's designed to handle smaller, faster transactions off the main network to reduce fees and speed things up. So, when I mentioned *main*, I was referring to the 'one and only' core Bitcoin network, which can be slower and expensive."

Bob's eyes widened as he prepared to share a particularly striking example, his tone carrying a mix of astonishment and concern. He paused for a moment, ensuring he had Alice's full attention before continuing. "It's quite eye-opening," he said, "in 2023, someone made a huge mistake and ended up paying around $3.1 million in fees—about 85 BTC—for a single transaction.[6] That was likely just human error, but it shows how high fees can get on the *main* network."

Alice's eyes widened in disbelief. "Wait, $3.1 million? In fees? That's insane!" She let out a short laugh, shaking her head. "I can't even wrap my head around that. How does something like that even happen? Honestly, that just makes me even more skeptical about

---

[6] Bitcoin Block 818,087.

using Bitcoin for regular transactions. If someone can accidentally pay that much in fees, it feels like a pretty risky system to rely on."

Bob nodded in agreement. "Let's just admit, compared to traditional finance, it's even more important for people who use crypto to be more cautious when making transactions. Now, we're about to dive into a bit more technical stuff. Are you ready?"

Alice nodded, her curiosity piqued. "Yes, please go ahead."

"Look, Alice, even though Bitcoin can be divided into tiny units like *satoshis*, the way transactions work in practice involves something called UTXOs," He began.

Alice looked curious. "Hold on, did you say U-T something or UFO? I'm not sure I'm hearing this right. What are those?"

Bob chuckled, a grin spreading across his face. "UFO? Well, that would definitely be out of this world. But no, it's U-T-X-O. It stands for *Unspent Transaction Output*. It's a bit less extraterrestrial but still quite interesting."

He continued, "UTXOs are essentially the 'chunks' of Bitcoin that you receive when you get Bitcoin from someone. Imagine these chunks as separate pieces of Bitcoin that you've collected over time. Each chunk is like a discrete amount of Bitcoin that you can spend, you don't actually split them into smaller parts."

"Remember we talked about Satoshi defining Bitcoin's *coin* as a *chain of digital signatures*? Sometimes, I find it more intuitive to visualize these UTXO chunks as the individual coins in our wallet. Just like physical coins, each UTXO is distinct, even though they all contribute to your total balance. Once you spend one, it's no longer available to spend again—just like if you gave someone a coin, you couldn't use it again yourself. So, when you think about spending Bitcoin, it's like you're picking out a coin or two from your collection of UTXOs to make a transaction."

Alice squinted in confusion, her expression mixing curiosity and amusement. "Hold on a sec, Bob," she said, with a playful tilt of her head. "First, you told me Bitcoin is like a giant pizza you can slice up, but now you're saying these 'UFO's cousins' are like uncut slices you can't break down further? How does that work? If I want to buy a coffee with Bitcoin, do I need to figure out how to split a UFO?"

Bob smiled, appreciating Alice's humor. "Nice one, Alice," he said. "Think of these 'UFO's cousins' like LEGO bricks. Each brick is a single piece you can't break apart, but you can stack and combine them to build whatever you need. Similarly, these Bitcoin chunks are indivisible chunks, but they can always be combined to make up any amount of Bitcoin you want. It's like having a dollar bill that you can't split, but you can use it along with other bills to cover any purchase. For example, if you want to buy something that costs $7, you would use a combination of a $5 bill and two $1 bills to pay. If you spend $7 with a $10 bill, you would get, let's say three $1 back in change."

He paused to let the analogy sink in. "Similarly, with Bitcoin, you can combine multiple Bitcoin chunks to create the exact amount you need for a transaction. Here's how it works: If you want to spend a small amount of Bitcoin, you'll end up using one or more of these Bitcoin chunks. For example, if you want to spend 1 Bitcoin but the only chunk you have is 1.5 Bitcoin, you would have to use that chunk of 1.5 Bitcoin for the transaction. The remaining amount, 0.5 Bitcoin, would be sent back to you as a new spendable chunk or even multiple smaller chunks. Keep in mind, transaction fees might also apply, so you would need to account for that."

Bob noticed that Alice looked puzzled. "When I mention 1.5 Bitcoin, I'm not talking about several smaller amounts that add up to 1.5 Bitcoin. Instead, imagine you have a single, solid piece of 1.5 Bitcoin—what I call a 'single spendable chunk.' You can't break this piece into smaller amounts during the transaction. You have to use the entire 1.5 Bitcoin at once."

He continued, "Now, how about another example? If you need to send 1 Bitcoin but only have multiple chunks of 0.5 Bitcoin and 0.3 Bitcoin, you would combine these chunks to cover the total amount. The network will process the entire amount, and any leftover Bitcoin after fees will be returned to you as spendable balances."

Alice thought for a moment and then said, "So, if I understand correctly, the network sort of 'gives back' any leftover Bitcoin after a transaction. I'm curious—do these returned amounts always come back as specific sizes, or can they be any size?"

Bob immediately realized that Alice might be visualizing those Bitcoin chunks as if they were like traditional money with fixed denominations. "In traditional currency, we're used to dealing with specific values, such as $10, $5, and $1 bills. However, in Bitcoin, these chunks aren't tied to any fixed amounts. Instead, the network handles Bitcoin in flexible amounts, so the sizes of the spendable chunks can vary and aren't predetermined like the denominations of physical money."

Alice's expression softened as Bob explained. She nodded slowly, her eyes brightening with understanding. "Ah, I get it now," she said, a thoughtful smile spreading across her face. She seemed to envision the concept more clearly, picturing it like using a mobile payment app where denominations don't matter. She tilted her head slightly, imagining how digital transactions work seamlessly without needing to deal with specific values like traditional bills and coins.

She tried to piece things together. "So, Bob, how does that work with my overall balance? If I have multiple chunks, how do they add up to show my total Bitcoin balance?" Her tone reflected that she was connecting the dots, but still seeking clarity.

Bob nodded, understanding the need for clarification. "That's a great point. The balance you see in your wallet isn't just a single number that reflects one chunk of Bitcoin. Instead, it's the total of all the spendable chunks associated with your wallet."

Alice tilted her head, intrigued. "So, my balance is actually made up of several 'UTXOs?'"

"Exactly," Bob confirmed. "Your wallet aggregates all the spendable chunks you've received and combines them to show your total balance. Each chunk is a discrete amount, but your wallet software sums up all these amounts to display your total Bitcoin balance. For instance, if you have chunks of 0.5 BTC, 0.2 BTC, and 0.3 BTC, your wallet will add these up to show a total balance of 1 BTC. Even though each UTXO is indivisible, the sum of all these chunks gives you your overall balance."

Alice frowned, looking more frustrated than before. "This all sounds really complicated, Bob. I can't imagine a regular Bitcoin user dealing with all these chunks and balances. Isn't it too complex for everyday use?"

Bob chuckled, trying to ease her frustration. "I understand it can seem complex at first, but the good news is that you don't have to deal with all these details yourself. The complexity is handled by your wallet software."

Alice looked relieved but curious. "So, I don't need to worry about managing UTXOs or anything like that?"

"No," Bob confirmed. "Your wallet does all the heavy lifting. It manages your UTXOs, calculates your total balance, and handles transactions. When you send or receive Bitcoin, the wallet takes care of selecting the right UTXOs, calculating change, and updating your balance. You just need to use the wallet interface to make transactions, and it handles the rest."

Alice nodded, feeling more at ease. "Oh, that's a relief. That makes things much clearer. It's good to know the wallet handles the complicated stuff. It sounds like this UTXO thingy is pretty central to how all cryptocurrencies work, huh?"

Bob smiled. "Actually, UTXOs are a key part of Bitcoin's design, but not all cryptocurrencies use this model. Some blockchains, like Ethereum, use different systems for managing transactions and balances. It's interesting to see how various digital currencies approach these challenges in their own ways."

Alice looked intrigued. "So, what are the other methods used?"

Bob explained, "Another common model is called the 'account-based model,' which is used by Ethereum. In this model, instead of dealing with UTXOs, each user has an account with a balance. When you make a transaction, the balance of the sender's account is reduced, and the balance of the receiver's account is increased. It's more like traditional banking systems, where you just see your balance and make transactions from that."

He continued. "In the account-based model, you don't have to worry about individual chunks of cryptocurrency. You just manage your account balance, and the system handles the details behind the scenes. Each model has its own advantages and fits different needs and use cases. But for most users, understanding the basics of how their wallet works is enough."

Alice nodded, starting to grasp the differences. "That's interesting. So, while Bitcoin uses the UTXO model, crypto projects like Ethereum use the account-based model. It's good to know there are different approaches out there."

Alice gazed out the café window, the bustling Tokyo street taking on a new clarity through her fresh perspective. She recognized that this was a paradigm shift, a fundamentally different way of thinking about money. It felt like she was seeing through the veil of traditional financial systems and uncovering a different reality that challenged everything she had assumed before.

Rules

Bob's attention was drawn to a delicate bracelet on Alice's wrist. The bracelet featured fine silver strands twisted into an elegant design, with a small, translucent gemstone at its center that caught the light, reflecting soft hues. However, as he looked closer, Bob noticed a slight imperfection—one of the silver strands was bent out of place, and the gemstone had a faint scratch across its surface.

"That's a beautiful bracelet," Bob commented, nodding toward her wrist. "But... looks like it's seen better days."

Alice smiled, though with a hint of frustration. She gently traced the scratch with her finger. "Yeah, I was really disappointed when it arrived like this. I bought it online from a boutique in Europe. It looked perfect in the pictures, but when it arrived, I saw the damage right away."

"Did you try to get it replaced?" Bob asked.

Alice sighed. "I did. That's when my refund and chargeback headache started. I reached out to the seller, but they didn't respond to my emails for weeks. It was so frustrating. In the end, I had to contact my credit card company to start a chargeback."

She shook her head as she recalled the ordeal. "The whole process took forever. The bank wanted me to provide proof of the damage, and then the seller finally got back to me after I filed the chargeback. It became a back-and-forth situation. At least I got my money back in the end, but it was way more hassle than it was worth."

Bob nodded sympathetically. "Yeah, chargebacks can be tricky. That's something Bitcoin doesn't have—once you send a payment, it reaches a point where it's practically non-reversible. I remember reading in one of Satoshi's earlier emails—he called it *sufficiently irreversible*.[7] There's no undoing it."

Alice's interest was piqued when she heard the term 'non-reversible.' She leaned in, her curiosity clearly sparked. "Non-reversible? That's a big deal. It sounds like once something is done on the blockchain, there's no going back, right? In traditional finance, we can often reverse transactions or fix mistakes, which gives us a safety net. But with crypto, it seems like there's a whole different level of finality?"

Her curiosity was evident—she was eager to understand how this concept differed from the more flexible nature of traditional financial systems, where transactions could often be reversed or corrected.

Bob smiled and said, "Yeah, 'non-reversible' is indeed an interesting feature of Bitcoin, and crypto in general. Basically, once a transaction is made, it can't be changed or recalled—it's locked in the very moment you hit send. The transaction is sealed and set in motion, completely out of your control, making it as 'final' as sending something into the past. It's different from traditional finance where you can often reverse transactions or address issues with banks. This feature of Bitcoin and most cryptocurrencies, while seemingly unforgiving, is actually essential to their security. It prevents tampering and fraud. However, it also means that, unlike traditional systems, there's no way to fix things if you make a mistake. There is simply no room for errors. So, it's just something to keep in mind when dealing with crypto."

Alice leaned in, thoughtfully. "I get that Bitcoin transactions are irreversible, but why would Satoshi think that's a good thing in the first place? For example, when I shop online, if I accidentally buy the wrong item or something goes wrong, I can usually get a refund or resolve the issue. With Bitcoin, once a transaction is done, there's

---

[7] Cryptography Mailing List. Satoshi Nakamoto's reply to James A. Donald. Subject: Bitcoin P2P e-cash paper. November 10, 2008.

no going back. What was the reason for making it so permanent? How does that actually help the system?"

Bob leaned in, wanting to make sure he explained this idea slowly and clearly. "Alice, I think we need to break this down carefully," he began. "When we say Bitcoin transactions are 'non-reversible,' it doesn't mean that if you buy something using Bitcoin and the seller messes up—like sending the wrong item or not delivering at all—you can't get a refund. You can still get your Bitcoin back, but only if the seller willingly gives it back to you."

He leaned back slightly, spreading his hands to emphasize the next point. "What we mean by 'non-reversible' is that there's no third party—like a bank or payment processor—that can cancel or reverse the transaction because they never had control over it to begin with. They also don't have custody of the funds. The only way the money comes back to you is if the person on the other side chooses to return it."

Bob continued, making sure to go step by step. "Now, there's another part to this idea of non-reversibility that's equally important to understand. Once a Bitcoin transaction is accepted into the blockchain by the majority, it's there permanently. No one can change or erase it. This is what we mean by *immutable*. It's locked in, forever. This is also why people say Bitcoin is *trustless*. You don't have to rely on a middleman like a bank or a third party to verify what happened. The record speaks for itself, and everyone can see it."

Bob paused, raising his hand slightly for emphasis. "But remember, this also means you need to be extra careful. Once you send Bitcoin, it's like throwing a die. There's no turning back. So, the responsibility is higher, but in return, you get a system that's truly transparent and decentralized."

He smiled, his eyes twinkling. "You know, it's hard to pinpoint exactly why Satoshi thought this was a good idea, but I think he really wanted to make transactions non-reversible to cut out the need for mediators in disputes."

"In the traditional finance world, banks and other institutions often have to step in to resolve issues between buyers and sellers, which can drive up transaction costs in several ways. For one, when a transaction goes wrong—like if a customer claims they never received a product—banks usually require evidence from both parties before making a decision. This often involves lengthy investigations, which can take time and resources."

"Because of these added steps, banks might charge higher fees for processing transactions or managing disputes. If you're a small business, these fees can stack up, making it less practical to sell low-cost items or offer casual services. For example, consider selling a $10 item online. If the transaction incurs a processing fee of around $0.60 (which includes a 3% fee plus a fixed cost), you end up losing a portion of your sale. Additionally, if there's a potential dispute, you might face a chargeback fee, which could add another $20 to $50 if the dispute isn't resolved in your favor. In this scenario, the total costs could significantly cut into your profit."

"Moreover, with the possibility of chargebacks or disputes, merchants have to be more cautious. They might need to collect more customer information to protect themselves, which can create privacy concerns. Customers may feel uncomfortable sharing personal details, like their address or phone number, especially if they're making small purchases. This can deter some people from completing a transaction, as they might not want to provide unnecessary information."

"By making Bitcoin transactions sufficiently irreversible, Satoshi aimed to simplify this whole process. Once a payment is made, it's done—there's no going back. This reduces the need for trust between buyers and sellers because both parties can feel secure knowing that the transaction is completed. Merchants can focus on their business instead of worrying about potential fraud or needing to deal with banks. This is a pretty big deal, and Satoshi made that vision pretty clear in the Bitcoin whitepaper."[8]

"While it might seem risky from a buyer's point of view, from a seller's side, it creates a lot of certainty. Imagine a buyer who intentionally tries to cheat the system. They might purchase something and then claim they never received it. With traditional payment methods like credit cards, they could dispute the charge and get their money back."

Alice frowned, clearly concerned. "I get that it's good for sellers to avoid chargebacks and fraud, but what if the seller isn't honest? If the seller never delivers what I paid for, there's no way to get it back. It feels like a huge risk for consumers. This whole non-reversible thing could really hurt people who don't fully understand the system or make honest mistakes."

Bob nodded, recognizing her concern. "It can seem like the system favors sellers since they don't have to worry about disputes or chargebacks. That's why it's so important to choose reputable sellers or merchants. Credible sellers have a strong incentive to maintain their reputation because their business relies on trust and positive reviews. They know that if they don't deliver as promised, they risk losing future customers and damaging their standing. While consumer protection laws do offer some safety, they primarily apply to legitimate businesses. If you deal with someone who isn't reputable, these protections might not help you, which is why sticking with trusted merchants is crucial."

He paused for a moment, then chuckled softly. "While nobody knows the real identity of Satoshi Nakamoto, I have this funny suspicion he must've had an online store somewhere and gotten fed up with all those chargebacks."

Bob chuckled again, leaning back as he explained his thought. "I mean, think about it. The whole system is designed in such a way

---

[8] Bitcoin: A Peer-to-Peer Electronic Cash System. Satoshi Nakamoto. Section 1: Introduction.

that once a transaction is made, it can't be reversed. That sounds like someone who's had enough of the traditional system where chargebacks could happen weeks after a sale. Maybe Satoshi—or whoever they are—ran an online business and just got tired of the headache that comes with chargebacks, fraud claims, and all the hoops sellers have to jump through to protect themselves."

He grinned, clearly enjoying his own theory. "It's almost like Bitcoin was designed with that frustration in mind. By making transactions final, it removes the constant worry for sellers about someone reversing a payment after they've already delivered a product. That's why I joke about Satoshi having some kind of online store—they probably had first-hand experience with the downsides of chargebacks."

Alice smiled at Bob's playful theory, her expression softening as she considered it. She could see where he was coming from. The idea made sense in a way—naturally, someone frustrated with the flaws in the traditional system might be driven to design something radically different.

Bob tilted his head, raising his hand slightly as if weighing things up. "Look, when it comes to dishonest sellers, it's not like you're completely safe even with regular money. The same thing can happen when you're shopping online with a credit card. Sure, there are protections, but they're not foolproof. If something goes wrong, there's no guarantee you'll get your money back. They help with disputes, but you're still relying on the seller to be honest. If they push back or say they sent the goods, you might still lose the chargeback. So, whether it's crypto or regular money, you're always taking some kind of risk."

"And it's not just about dealing with sellers or merchants, either. The same idea applies when you're sending Bitcoin between your own wallets." He gestured with his hands, emphasizing the point. "If you send it to the wrong address, there's no intermediary to fix that mistake. It's all on you."

Alice looked a bit puzzled and asked, "But what could go wrong when sending Bitcoin between your own wallets? It sounds pretty safe, since it's just moving it around within your own accounts."

Bob smiled, appreciating Alice's curiosity. "It does sound pretty safe, right? But there are still a few things that can go wrong. For example, if you accidentally send Bitcoin to the wrong address, there's no way to reverse the transaction. Once it's sent, it's out of your control. Also, if you lose access to one of your wallets, you might lose access to the Bitcoin in that wallet forever. It's important to be meticulous and cautious, even when dealing with your own wallets, to avoid any potential issues."

Alice sighed, clearly not impressed. "I get the need for security and how it helps sellers, but the idea that mistakes can't be undone feels pretty risky for consumers. It's definitely a big drawback in my book."

Bob nodded thoughtfully, drawing from his own experience. "But think about it—there are plenty of real-life situations where mistakes can't be undone either. A while ago, I was working on a project and accidentally deleted an important file. I thought I could restore it from a backup later, but it turned out the backup was incomplete, and I lost a lot of crucial work. I mean, sometimes having the option to fix mistakes can make people a bit careless because they know they can fix it later if needed."

Alice listened to Bob's story and a flicker of recognition crossed her face. "That reminds me of something that happened to me a few years ago. I accidentally deleted a whole batch of old photos from my phone—pictures from my family's vacation to Italy. We had visited all these beautiful spots, like the Amalfi Coast and the Colosseum, and I thought they were backed up in the cloud. But when I went to recover them, they were just… gone. I hadn't synced my phone properly, and those photos were lost forever."

She sighed, her expression softening a bit. "It still stings, knowing they're gone because of a simple mistake. I guess I see your point now. When there's no option to undo something, it really makes you think twice before acting. But it's still tough, knowing that kind of caution is required with every little transaction in crypto."

Alice crossed her arms, thinking out loud. "Maybe the safest way to spend Bitcoin is to use it in person—buy something and get it right there on the spot. At least that way, you know you're getting what you paid for immediately."

Bob smiled and nodded, "Yeah, that's a smart approach. When you're face-to-face, you cut down on a lot of the risks. But for online transactions, you could always rely on an *escrow* service. That way, the payment is held until both parties are satisfied. It adds a layer of protection, even though you're still dealing with Bitcoin's non-reversible nature."

Alice's brow furrowed slightly as she latched onto the new term.

"Escrow? I've heard the word before, but I've never really understood how it works. How does an escrow service actually help in Bitcoin or crypto transactions?"

Bob took his time, choosing his words carefully. "Alright, think of escrow like a neutral third party in a transaction. Let's say you're buying something expensive, like a car. Instead of just handing over the money and hoping the seller delivers, you both put your trust in this middle person, or service, who holds the money until the deal is completed. Once both you and the seller are satisfied, the escrow service releases the funds."

"Without escrow, things can get a bit messier. Let's say you're dealing with a stranger on the other side of the world, and you have no idea if they're legit. If there's no middleman to hold the money, what's stopping the seller from taking your cash and vanishing? Or, if you're the seller, how do you know the buyer isn't going to just disappear once they have the goods?"

He leaned forward slightly to make sure Alice was following. "In the case of crypto, it works similarly. The crypto, let's say Bitcoin, gets held by the escrow service until both parties—buyer and seller—are happy with the deal. That way, there's a bit of extra security in case something goes wrong. It's not a perfect solution, but it's better than blindly trusting the other person in a transaction."

Alice furrowed her brow, clearly catching something that didn't sit right with her. "Wait a second," she said, sitting up a little straighter. "Isn't the whole point of making transactions non-reversible to get rid of intermediaries? You know, to bring down costs and simplify things? But now, with escrow, we're introducing a middleman again, which seems like it's going against that whole idea. Aren't we back to square one with this? If we need a third party to make sure things go smoothly, how is this really different from the traditional system?"

Bob took a moment to gather his thoughts. "I get your point about escrow services introducing an intermediary, which seems to contradict the original vision of Bitcoin," he began, his voice steady and reflective.

"Let's think about this a bit more. In traditional money transactions, intermediaries are necessary to handle things like online payments and resolving disputes—it's an inseparable part of the system. And, let's not forget. Escrow is not a crypto-specific term. Many transactions in traditional finance also rely on escrow services to manage risk upfront, especially in high-value or sensitive deals. Now, with Bitcoin and many other cryptocurrencies, transactions can be carried out directly between users, meaning there's no need for a middleman at all, with or without escrow service."

"Besides, there's a key distinction between the role of intermediaries in traditional finance and escrow services in the crypto world. In traditional finance, intermediaries like banks and credit card companies often step in after something has gone wrong—like fraud or a dispute. They act as a *corrective* measure, resolving issues after they occur, and in some cases, they profit from the very problems they're addressing through fees or other charges. Escrow services, on the other hand, focus on *prevention*. Their role is to manage risk before any issues arise, acting as a safeguard to ensure both parties in a transaction fulfill their obligations before the deal goes through. So, while both intermediaries and escrow services offer oversight, escrow is all about preventing disputes upfront, whereas traditional intermediaries deal with problems after the fact—a clear difference between *prevention* and *correction*."

He smiled slightly, trying to clarify his stance further. "Moreover, unlike chargebacks with credit cards, where the cost of fraud or disputes is often absorbed by the financial institutions and indirectly passed on to users through fees, escrow services place the responsibility directly on the transaction parties. If you're using escrow, you're choosing to pay for that added layer of security because you recognize the risk involved. It's a more transparent way of avoiding potential disputes, and you're fully aware of the costs and benefits before engaging in the transaction."

"So, while escrow might seem like it adds an intermediary, it's not a feature built-into Bitcoin. Instead, it is actually more about giving users options and control over their transactions. It's about handling risks in a way that's upfront and agreed upon, rather than, I would say, a hidden agenda like with traditional financial systems."

Alice took a moment to absorb Bob's explanations, her expression reflecting a mix of contemplation and clarity. She thought back to her initial concern about escrow services introducing an intermediary, which seemed at odds with the original vision of Bitcoin to eliminate middlemen.

Her thoughts buzzed as she pieced things together. First, Bitcoin operates absolutely fine without intermediaries like escrow—it's all about direct transactions between individuals. In contrast, traditional finance relies heavily on banks and other intermediaries, which are essential for its smooth functioning. Escrow services, on the other hand, can be used as a safeguard for larger or more complex transactions, helping to prevent issues before they happen. This is quite different from the role of banks, which usually step in only after a problem arises, like when they handle credit card chargebacks.

Her mind spun with a new theory: *What if* banks quietly benefit from letting some fraud slip through? Not intentionally, but maybe they're not too worried about catching everything right away. If cardholders miss the fraud and don't request a chargeback in time, the bank still profits from processing and late fees. Sure, they handle chargebacks, but the cost might be less than what they make from customers who don't notice fraud. The system, meant to protect consumers, might also allow banks to avoid dealing with their own security flaws. In the end, everyone benefits—except the merchants.

She then recalled her own experience of unauthorized credit card use. It took her almost a month to notice, and she quickly called the bank. They issued a temporary credit, adjusting her balance. At the time, she was relieved and thankful.

But now, reflecting on her conversation with Bob, she realized something crucial. That temporary credit wasn't real money—it was just a digital adjustment. The bank simply changed the numbers on her balance. While this adjustment spared her from paying the fraudulent charges, no physical money was exchanged. The bank manipulated account figures to temporarily erase the charge from her balance.

She understood now why the bank could handle this so effortlessly. If the seller accepted the chargeback, the fraudulent charge would disappear permanently. If the seller won, her balance would return, and she would owe the money. In either case, neither the bank nor the thief lost anything.

As her thoughts swirled, Alice began to feel the weight of her internal conflict. The chargeback had saved her, but the merchant bore the financial hit. The system had shielded her, shifting the burden onto someone else.

She questioned her role in this. By continuing to use credit cards, she was participating in a system that protected her while leaving merchants to suffer the consequences. On the surface, it seemed fair—she had been the victim of fraud—but the solution wasn't as simple as it appeared.

She valued the chargeback protection; it felt like a safety net in the uncertain world of online transactions. Yet, the unfairness gnawed at her. Was her peace of mind worth the cost to small businesses and independent sellers? She wondered how often they had to deal with the fallout from someone else's mistake or dishonesty, losing revenue while consumers like her walked away unscathed.

Guilt crept in, but part of her wasn't ready to give up the protection. Why should she sacrifice the shield that protected her from fraud, especially when chargebacks seemed like such a minimal inconvenience for banks? It was easier to look the other way, feeling it wasn't her responsibility to fix the system. Even though the system's flaws bothered her, it gave her security she wasn't ready to lose.

The dilemma ran deeper than she had expected. Her self-interest pulled her in one direction, while a growing awareness of the system's inequities tugged her in another. She was left uneasy, unsure where to land. Could she justify staying in a flawed system for the sake of convenience, or did her peace of mind come at too high a moral cost?

The idea of irreversible transactions had lingered since they discussed how Bitcoin works without intermediaries. But something about it still unsettled her, especially when compared to traditional payment systems.

After a brief pause, she voiced her thoughts. "Bob, here's something I'm wondering: when you use a mobile payment app or make a direct bank transfer, you don't really get chargeback options like you do with a credit card. In those cases, it's pretty much like a non-reversible transaction. So, doesn't that make those payment methods similar to Bitcoin in terms of finality? Why do we even need Bitcoin?" she asked, her curiosity tinged with skepticism.

Bob nodded, listening carefully before responding. "I get why you would think that—they do seem similar on the surface. But they're really not the same at all. With a bank transfer or a mobile payment app, you typically don't have the same chargeback options as you do with a credit card. But banks can still step in if something goes wrong. They can freeze your account, reverse certain transactions, or even intervene if they suspect fraud. With Bitcoin, none of that is possible. Once a transaction is made, it's final. No one can step in to reverse it or freeze your assets. So, while they seem alike because of the lack of chargebacks, they're fundamentally different in how much control the system has over your money."

He paused, gathering his thoughts. "Moreover, I could go on about the various benefits that Bitcoin and other cryptocurrencies offer. There are definitely ways in which they can be seen as superior to traditional systems. But right now, it's not so much about saying one is better than the other. The point is that Bitcoin and crypto provide valuable alternatives that address some of the limitations we see in conventional financial methods. It's really not about declaring one as perfect and the other as flawed—it's about recognizing that each has its own strengths and weaknesses and offering choices to fit different needs."

Alice took a moment to absorb Bob's response, her mind churning with the implications. Bitcoin's non-reversibility, she realized, might feel unforgiving in its finality, but it also introduced a different level of directness, transparency, and immutability.

The contrast between the comfort of chargebacks and the fairness of decentralized systems like Bitcoin struck her deeply. She found herself grappling with the design and intent behind these systems. Traditional financial methods had their own set of advantages, but they were often built on a foundation that could be biased or opaque.

In contrast, Bitcoin's design, with its focus on decentralization and transparency, aimed to protect users in a different way. It removed intermediaries and allowed for direct interactions, but it also meant that users had to navigate risks more independently. Alice couldn't help but question which system was truly more fair in the long run.

The serene atmosphere of the Tokyo café was momentarily disrupted by a ripple of disquietude. A businessman, his composure visibly strained, exchanged terse words with a young barista over a spilled matcha latte. The barista, bowing deeply in apology and swiftly wiping at the mess, attempted to defuse the situation. The businessman, however, his face etched with silent disapproval, with a hint of a bow acknowledging the apology, deposited a damp bill on the counter and exited the café with a barely audible murmur.

Alice watched the scene unfold with a flicker of surprise in her eyes. "That poor barista," she said softly, turning back to Bob.

Bob chuckled, a touch of amusement softening his features. "The occasional spill, I'm afraid, is part of the café experience. Now, back to more questions from you, Alice..." He gestured for her to continue.

Alice stirred her iced Americano, the clinking of the straw against the glass the only sound in the brief lull of their conversation. A mischievous glint sparked in her eyes after Bob's invitation for more questions.

"So, anyone can see everything on this blockchain ledger, right?" she asked, leaning forward. "Transactions, balances, the whole shebang?"

Bob chuckled, taking a sip of his Americano. "Pretty much," he replied. "Transparency is one of the big selling points of blockchain technology."

Alice's smile grew, a playful glint in her eyes. "Transparency can be fun," she teased. "But what if I didn't like the amount in someone else's account? Couldn't I just... change it?"

Bob raised an eyebrow, a smile still playing on his lips. "Hold on there, Alice," he said gently. "It's not quite that simple. There's this thing called a *consensus mechanism*, which is like a set of rules that keeps everyone honest. Think of it like a group project – everyone has to agree on the final version before it's official."

"For example, Bitcoin's rules provide a framework about how Bitcoin transactions are verified, compiled into a data block, accepting the data block to be subsequently added to the blockchain, and selecting the longest chain. Essentially, it's about agreeing on which and how crypto transactions can be added to the official record."

"So, you are saying these rules create some sort of order?" Alice asked, intrigued.

"Precisely," Bob responded.

"Hold on a sec, Bob," Alice interrupted, a flicker of further confusion crossing her face. "You said there's no single ruler in a decentralized system, but then you mentioned consensus mechanisms being the rules. Aren't those kind of like a central authority, dictating how things work, a ruler in disguise?"

Bob smiled, recognizing Alice's astute observation. "Here's the key difference: consensus mechanisms aren't enforced by a single entity. Think of them more like pre-programmed guidelines written into the code of the blockchain itself. Everyone who participates in the network agrees to follow these guidelines *voluntarily*. The mechanisms themselves don't have any real power. They simply provide a framework for how everyone collectively decides on things. There's no central authority to punish you if you break the rules, but the network itself might reject your actions or exclude you from participating."

"But doesn't rejecting my actions or excluding me sound like a form of punishment? It feels like I'm being punished for not playing by the rules." She pursed her lips, her eyes narrowing slightly as she pondered the implications.

"It's more like a natural consequence than a punishment," Bob replied, a thoughtful expression on his face. "Imagine you're playing a game and you break the rules. The game doesn't exactly punish you, but it just doesn't let you keep playing." He paused, raising his hands in a shrugging motion, as if illustrating the game's response.

"It's the same with Bitcoin. The network is just enforcing the rules that everyone agreed on. Picture it as a self-regulating system. If someone tries to cheat, the system automatically adjusts to correct itself and keep everything fair."

Alice's face flushed with embarrassment as she realized her earlier question might have seemed a bit off. Her cheeks turning pink. She chuckled softly, looking down at her coffee. "I guess I was overthinking it. It's not about trying to break the rules and still stay in the system. That doesn't really make sense." She gave a small, awkward smile, feeling a bit silly for asking what now seemed like a bit of a clueless question.

Bob noticed Alice's embarrassment and offered a reassuring smile. "Hey, don't worry about it," he said warmly. "It's totally okay to ask questions, even if they feel a bit off. It's all part of figuring things out. Everyone has moments like that." He gave a reassuring nod, hoping to ease her discomfort.

Bob's reassuring words definitely helped Alice feel a bit more at ease. She took a deep breath and refocused on the topic at hand. "Thanks, Bob," she said with a renewed sense of curiosity.

"So, if we're talking about how the system keeps itself in check, does that mean these consensus mechanisms are kind of like the constitution of a decentralized system?" She asked, hoping to solidify her understanding of how these mechanisms fit into the broader picture.

"An interesting analogy," Bob mused. "They are foundational rules, yes, but perhaps not as rigid as a constitution. The beauty of some consensus mechanisms is that they can be changed, as long as the community agrees to the changes."

"So, it's an evolving set of rules?" Alice asked, her curiosity piqued.

"Yup," Bob replied. "The world of consensus mechanisms is fascinating and constantly developing"

He paused, a thoughtful expression crossing his face. "There are actually quite a few different ways to achieve consensus. Want to dive into some examples?"

Alice sat up straighter, her hands clasped together. "Absolutely! Let's do it."

Bob leaned back in his chair and began, "In many systems, especially ones involving valuable assets or sensitive information, there's always a risk of someone trying to cheat or manipulate the process for their own gain. Imagine a system where anyone could just step in and change the records, or even flood it with fake entries. That would lead to chaos—no one would know what to trust, and the system would break down."

Alice nodded, following along. "Yeah, that sounds like a huge problem. If anyone can tamper with the records, there's no real security."

"Exactly," Bob agreed. "So, to solve this, you need a way to make sure that no one can just walk in and change things. For example, you can require participants to prove their commitment to the system—something that shows they've invested real effort before they're allowed to add anything new. This effort has to be costly, in terms of resources like time and computational power, so it's not something that can be faked or done lightly."

Alice's eyes lit up with understanding. "Ah, so you're making it hard for people to mess with the system by requiring them to put in significant work first. That way, only those who are serious and have something to lose will be able to contribute?"

"Exactly," Bob replied. "This approach ensures that any contribution to the system comes from someone who has already put in a lot of effort. It makes cheating or manipulation much less appealing because the cost to do so is just too high."

Bob leaned forward, continuing from where he left off. "This is where the concept of *Proof of Work* comes in."

Alice raised her eyebrows. "Proof-of-Work? Is that what it's called?"

"Yes," Bob confirmed. "The idea is simple but powerful. For example, by making participants solve a difficult puzzle computationally, they prove they've invested enough data-crunching work, electricity-hungry effort, and time—kind of like spending money. The more computational power they use, the more they *invest* in the process. Only then can they contribute to the system."

Alice nodded slowly, connecting the dots. "So this is the method that ensures participants have skin in the game before they can make changes. It's like a built-in protection against manipulation?"

"Exactly," Bob said. "It's a way to create trust without needing to rely on a central authority. The work itself becomes the proof that everything is being done legitimately."

Alice leaned in, intrigued. "Okay, I think I get it. But what's this Proof of Work got to do with Bitcoin?"

Bob smiled. "Well, it's pretty straightforward—Bitcoin, and a bunch of other cryptos, use the Proof of Work concept to make sure that only those who put in the effort can add new records—new data blocks—to the blockchain. Remember, when someone sends Bitcoin to someone else, the details of that transaction are grouped with others and placed into a *block*."

"But before we go any further, let's look at how the Bitcoin network works. Network participants who compete to add data blocks to the blockchain are known as the *miners*. Miners around the world are constantly working to propose the next immediate block to be added to the Bitcoin blockchain. To qualify for adding a block, they must prove they have done enough computational work by solving a complex cryptographic puzzle using their computers— a process known as *mining*, which is essentially how proof of work is put into action. Given they are all working separately, it's possible that two or more miners could successfully solve the puzzle at almost the same time. That being said, they aren't creating identical blocks because each one might include different sets of transactions. Once a miner's block is ready, they broadcast it to the network. This starts a race. The block that the majority accepts becomes the official one, and miners can then begin working on the next block using that version as the new starting point. In that sense, Bitcoin's system works pretty much like a *majority rules* decision, but unlike social norms that can be swayed by emotions, the agreement here is purely driven by evidence of computational work. The blocks that don't make it, known as *stale* blocks, are discarded. However, their transactions aren't lost—those transactions simply wait to be added to a future block."

"If some miners somehow decided to keep building on a specific stale block, they could stage a sort of *coup*, splitting off and create a new chain—a *fork*, with a shared history with the original Bitcoin blockchain up until the split but a separate future from that point onward. By the way, a fork in the network can occur for other reasons too. For example, if there's a disagreement over protocol changes—like when *Bitcoin Cash* split from Bitcoin—it's a deliberate decision by a group of miners and nodes to follow different rules."

He continued. "Anyway, the miner who successfully adds a valid data block to the *longest chain* gets some *newly minted* Bitcoins as a *reward*. In case you're wondering, the *longest chain* is basically the one that has the most blocks in it. It's not just about length, though—it's about the chain with the most *work* done on it. Remember, every time a miner adds a block, they're solving a complex puzzle that requires a lot of computational effort, or energy. The more blocks a chain has, the more work has gone into it. The reason this matters is that the Bitcoin blockchain is decentralized, meaning no central authority is in charge. So, the *longest chain* is seen as the most trustworthy version of the transaction history because it represents the chain with the most effort, and, therefore, the most security."

Alice furrowed her brow and leaned in slightly, clearly puzzled. "Wait a minute, I'm a bit confused. What exactly do you mean by *newly minted* Bitcoins?"

Bob grinned and leaned back, holding his hands up. "When I say 'newly minted,' I mean that the Bitcoin protocol creates *brand-new* Bitcoins. The system *releases* a set amount of fresh Bitcoins to any miner who successfully solves the puzzle. The tricky part is that while the miner can claim those coins, that doesn't make them 'official' just yet. They only become part of the total Bitcoin supply once other miners verify and accept the block into the longest chain. Until then, those coins aren't fully recognized on the network."

But how, Alice wondered, could the constant creation of new Bitcoins align with the fixed supply of 21 million? Her eyes narrowed slightly as she stared into space, lost in thought.

Bob noticed her sudden shift of expression. "I can see you're thinking something doesn't quite add up?"

Alice nodded. "Yeah, if the total supply is fixed at 21 million, how does it make sense that miners keep getting new Bitcoins? Doesn't that seem to go against the idea of a fixed supply?"

Bob leaned in, eager to clarify. "The trick here is to understand the concept of 'circulating supply.' Even though the total Bitcoin supply is capped at 21 million, not all of those Bitcoins are available in the market right now. While Bitcoin's total supply is capped, but new Bitcoins are introduced slowly through the mining process."

Alice nodded, starting to understand. "Okay, so you are saying the new Bitcoins are part of the 21 million cap?"

Bob smiled, glad she was following along. "Precisely. The newly minted Bitcoins are included in that 21 million total. As time goes on, the total number of Bitcoins will eventually reach 21 million and not go beyond it."

Alice's eyes sparkled with curiosity. "So when will this total of 21 million be reached?"

Bob paused for a moment before saying, "The last Bitcoin is expected to be *mined* around 2140. Oh, and by the way, there's a reason we call that process 'mining.' Satoshi actually thought of it like this: just as gold miners put in effort and resources to dig up gold, the process of adding new Bitcoins is kind of the same. It's all about using resources to bring those coins into the market."

"That's fascinating!" Alice exclaimed. "So miners are like digital gold prospectors, but instead of digging in the mountains of *La Rinconada*, they're sifting through the virtual world to uncover hidden treasure. Though, thinking about it… *La Rinconada* is kind of 'lawless' in a way, right? Yet even in that chaos, the miners still follow their own set of rules. I guess the same goes for Bitcoin miners—there's no central authority, but they're still bound by the rules of the network to keep everything running smoothly. By the way, Bob, how many new Bitcoins does a miner get if they successfully mine a block today? I feel like I should know this, but it's never really come up."

Bob smiled, realizing they hadn't touched on this yet. "Right now, a successful Bitcoin miner gets 3.125 Bitcoins every time they add a new block to the Bitcoin blockchain."

Alice's eyes widened a little. That sounds like a fortune. With Bitcoin's current price around $60,000, that's over $180,000!"

Bob chuckled. "It does, doesn't it? But here's the thing—they used to get way more than that. When Bitcoin first started, miners were earning 50 Bitcoins for every block they mined."

Alice nearly spat out her coffee. "Fifty?! That's a huge difference!"

"Yep," Bob said, nodding. " But keep in mind, fifty Bitcoins were worth only a few dollars back then. A lot of people didn't think much of it—they either spent or lost them without a second thought. If they had held onto them, though…" He trailed off, shaking his head with a knowing grin. "Well, let's just say those few dollars would've turned into millions today.

He paused for a moment, then added, "So, here's the thing about Bitcoin. Bitcoin has this thing called *halving*. After every 210,000 Bitcoin blocks—roughly every four years, though it's not exactly precise because we're talking about block time, not calendar time—the reward for mining gets cut in half. After the first halving back in 2012, the reward dropped from 50 to 25, then 12.5, 6.25 and now we're at 3.125 per block. It's kind of like Bitcoin's version of a *leap year*—though instead of adjusting the calendar, it adjusts the reward."

Alice leaned back, processing what Bob had said. "So, the rewards get smaller over time? Why would it work like that?"

Bob nodded. "Yeah, that's what most people notice—the miners' rewards keep getting lesser. And they're not wrong, but how about we look at it from a different angle? I could be wrong, but I think Satoshi's plan was to make it really appealing for miners to jump in early, especially when Bitcoin was just starting out. At the same time, he needed to keep them motivated to stick around for the long haul."

Bob continued, "Think about it. In the early days, Bitcoin was this completely new concept, and Satoshi needed people—miners—to get involved, to actually secure the network and validate transactions. Without miners, the whole system wouldn't work. So, offering higher rewards at the beginning was a way to make it really appealing for them to take that risk and invest their time and resources in something that wasn't even proven yet."

"By giving them bigger rewards at first, Satoshi was basically saying, 'Hey, help get this thing off the ground, and you'll be well compensated.' But he also knew those rewards couldn't stay high forever."

Alice looked curious. "But why not just keep the incentives high forever? Wouldn't that keep everyone happy?"

Bob smiled. "Well, remember, Bitcoin has a hard cap of 21 million coins. That's all there will ever be. And the only way to create and release those Bitcoins into the hands of the community is through mining rewards. If the rewards stayed high 'forever,' we would run out of reward for the miners way too quickly blowing through the supply too fast. That could really stunt the network's growth and make it harder for Bitcoin to gain traction. It's like he was giving Bitcoin room to grow and mature, ensuring it had time to dominate."

Alice tilted her head, a bit confused. "Wait, what do you mean by the *only* way to create and release those Bitcoins into circulation is through mining rewards? Isn't there another way they could be released?"

Bob grinned, recognizing the familiar question. "Yeah, I know it sounds a bit weird at first. So yes, mining is the *only* way they come into existence. It's all part of the reward system for miners. If it helps, you could even picture mining like a digital 3D printer that cranks out shiny new Bitcoins in the digital realm."

"And if you want to think about it a bit differently, you could say that miners 'write Bitcoin into existence'—just in a metaphorical way, of course," Bob explained. "Every time they solve those complex problems, they're adding new Bitcoin to the ledger—literally making it exist by recording it in the blockchain. It's like they're writing it into reality with each block they add."

Alice frowned, trying to piece it together. "So basically, if no one mines, no new Bitcoin gets made?"

"Exactly," Bob said, nodding. "If mining were to just stop today, we wouldn't see any new Bitcoins being created. So, Bitcoin would never hit its maximum supply. In a way, these miners act like the 'official distributors' of Bitcoin," he added with a chuckle.

Alice raised an eyebrow, curious. "What if those miners decide to keep the Bitcoin to themselves? How would that affect the market?"

Bob thought for a moment. "That's a good question. If miners hoard their Bitcoin instead of selling it, it could lead to a few different outcomes. First, if a lot of Bitcoin is taken out of circulation and kept by miners, it would reduce the supply available on exchanges. With less Bitcoin available for buying, demand could push the price up.

He continued, "On the flip side, if miners hold onto their Bitcoin for too long and don't sell, they might miss out on potential profits when prices rise. The market operates on supply and demand, so if everyone starts holding instead of selling, it could create tension between current market prices and what people are willing to pay."

Alice nodded slowly, absorbing the implications. "So, to a certain extent, their decisions could really impact how Bitcoin behaves in the market?"

"Exactly," Bob replied. "It's a balancing act. If everyone believes Bitcoin is valuable and holds onto it, that could drive prices up, but if too many miners decide to sell at once, it could flood the market and push prices down."

Bob pulled out his phone and quickly checked the numbers. "Here's something interesting: mining companies hold about 9% of the total Bitcoin supply. And when you include institutions—like crypto exchanges, private and public companies, governments, and funds like ETFs—around 43% of all Bitcoin is in their hands.[9] So while miners do hold a significant chunk, they're just one piece of a much larger puzzle when it comes to Bitcoin distribution."

Alice trying hard to grasp the concept. "It would be great if more people started mining—that way everything would just speed up, just like adding more workers to speed up production in a factory."

Bob replied with a smile, "You might think that more miners would make transactions faster, but that's not exactly how it works. In the Bitcoin network, a new data block carrying transaction details is created roughly every 10 minutes. This timing doesn't change, no matter how many miners are working. When more miners join, the puzzle they solve to create a block becomes harder. It's like a video game increasing in difficulty as you level up. The system is designed

---

[9] https://www.grayscale.com/research/reports/demystifying-bitcoins-ownership-landscape. Last update: November 30, 2023. Accessed: October 23, 2024.

this way to keep the creation of new blocks steady, around one every 10 minutes. Likewise, if the process ever takes longer than usual, the network adjusts by making the puzzle easier so that miners can still find blocks within that 10-minute window."

"But why is a delay necessary at all? Why ten minutes? Isn't faster usually better? Why not just create the blocks as quickly as possible without slowing things down?" Alice fired off questions, her curiosity bubbling over as she tilted her head.

Bob leaned forward, focusing on how to explain it to her. "As new blocks get added, the blockchain gets bigger, and if blocks were created too fast, the whole system could grow out of control. Imagine if your computer had to store all that information—eventually, it would run out of space or slow down. That's probably how and why the ten-minute block time was initially conceived—it's like a buffer to keep things steady."[10]

Bob continued, "It turns out this delay actually helps the network in some important ways too. When someone makes a transaction, that information has to be shared with everyone on the network so they can update their records. If new blocks were added too quickly, some users might not get the update before the next one is created, which could lead to confusion or, worse, *double spending*. It's like trying to have a conversation in a noisy room—if too many people are talking at once, you can't hear anything clearly. The ten-minute wait ensures everyone has enough time to catch up."

Alice raised an eyebrow, clearly skeptical. "Okay, but if I were a miner, I wouldn't be too thrilled about spending 10 minutes competing with everyone else only to find out I lost the game. That seems like a lot of wasted effort. Why even bother?"

Bob smiled and gently corrected her. "Actually, it doesn't take 10 minutes for everyone to know a new block has been found. Today, it only takes a few seconds for about 90% of the network to get the

---

[10] Bitcoin: A Peer-to-Peer Electronic Cash System. Satoshi Nakamoto. Section 7: Reclaiming Disk Space.

news.[11] Once most of the network knows, they can stop wasting their energy on that block and move on to the next one. It's really not as bad as it sounds. The few seconds you 'waste' are just a part of making sure the network stays coordinated and no one tries to double spend."

Alice asked, "What's this *double spending* all about?"

Bob smiled, sensing an opportunity to clarify. "Imagine I sent you a Bitcoin, and almost immediately, I also tried to send that exact same Bitcoin to someone else. That's double spending in a nutshell."

Alice frowned, remembering an earlier conversation. "But wait, you told me before that Bitcoin transactions are *irreversible*. Once it's sent, it's gone, right? How could someone even try to send the same Bitcoin twice?"

Bob leaned forward, trying to clear things up. "Alright, Alice, I get why it sounds confusing. *Double-spending* and *irreversibility* might seem related, but they're actually two different concepts."

"Imagine you have two checks. You write both checks to pay for the same item. If you were to mail both checks, there's a chance that both could be cashed, even though you only have enough money to cover one of them. This would be a form of *double-spending*."

"In the context of cryptocurrency, when someone tries a double-spend, they're essentially racing to get one version of a transaction confirmed over another before either is finalized. But once the network confirms a transaction and includes it in the blockchain, it's locked in—that's what we mean by 'irreversible.' So, *double-spending* is an attempt to make two competing versions of a transaction, but only one can ever make it onto the blockchain. Once it does, the other is discarded, and that confirmed transaction can't be undone."

He paused, checking her reaction. "So, simply put, *double-spending* is about trying to get away with spending the same *coin* or

---

[11] https://www.dsn.kastel.kit.edu/bitcoin/#propagation

token twice, while *irreversibility* means that once a transaction is confirmed, there's no going back."

Alice tilted her head, catching on to Bob's phrasing. "Wait, so when you say *coin* and *token*, you're talking about two different things? I thought they were just different words for the same thing."

Bob saw a chance to clarify another point. "Oh, and since we're on this topic, I should mention—people in the crypto community actually make a distinction between *coins* and *tokens*," he said.

"A *coin*, like Bitcoin, is usually tied to its own blockchain. It's kind of like the *native currency* of that specific network—Bitcoin belongs to the Bitcoin blockchain, for instance. A *token*, though, is different. It's built on top of an existing blockchain, like Ethereum. Tokens aren't tied to a single blockchain the way coins are; they're more like digital assets or units that can represent a lot of things—anything from ownership in a project to access to certain features within an app."

He paused, gauging her interest. "So, think of *coins* as the currency of their own blockchain networks, while *tokens* are more like flexible assets built on top of other blockchains."

Alice frowned, a bit puzzled. "Wait, Bob," she said, "you keep saying 'the *same* coin.' But isn't it like cash? I mean, if I have two ten-dollar bills, I wouldn't think of them as different. I wouldn't say I've spent the 'same' ten-dollar bill if I just use another one. So how does that work with Bitcoin? I thought one Bitcoin is just like any other, right?" She tilted her head, trying to make sense of it.

Bob leaned back and smiled, noticing Alice's puzzled look. "Ah, I see where the confusion is. When I say 'the *same* coin,' I'm not talking about two identical, physical coins like you might think of with traditional money. Remember those UTXOs, the Bitcoin chunks—the *UFO's cousins* of your version?" He chuckled. "So, when I mention 'the *same* coin,' I'm referring to trying to spend the same UTXO again, even though it's already been used."

Alice nodded slowly, thinking it over. "Okay, I think I get it now. It's like having a concert ticket with a unique barcode. Once I scan it at the entrance, I can't just print another copy and expect to get in with the 'same' ticket. Even if the ticket looks identical, it's already been used and recorded."

"That's definitely an interesting analogy to look at it," Bob nodded and continued. "Alright, back to *double spending*. There's still a lot more to unpack here, so here's how it would potentially work in practice: You buy something with Bitcoin, and you know it takes at least 10 minutes for the transaction to be included in the blockchain—sometimes even longer. Imagine you manage to trick the seller into thinking you've sent the Bitcoin, using some clever deception. They believe you and deliver the product right away, even though the transaction clearly hasn't been included in the Bitcoin blockchain yet. But here's the catch: you've secretly created another Bitcoin transaction using that same Bitcoin, this time sending it to your own wallet, without the seller knowing."

"As someone controlling the majority of mining power, you make sure the second transaction, the one that sends the Bitcoin back to yourself, gets included in the blockchain *first*. The first transaction, the one meant for the seller, is ignored by the network because based on the official record, that Bitcoin has already been spent. From the seller's perspective, they're still waiting for their payment, while you're sitting there with the item and the Bitcoin. You keep stringing them along, telling them the network is just slow or congested, and by the time they realize what's happened, it's too late—the fraudulent transaction sending Bitcoin to your own wallet is *buried deep* in the blockchain."

"When I talk about it being 'buried deep,' I'm really referring to how far down in the blockchain that fraudulent transaction goes. Let's put it in perspective: we know it takes about 10 minutes to add a new block, after 3 days, we're looking at over 400 blocks stacked on top of your transaction. At that point, it's like trying to dig up a treasure that's been buried for years. To reverse it, someone would have to go back and redo all the work for every one of those blocks, which is basically impossible. By the time anyone realizes what happened, that fraudulent transaction is already locked in tight within the blockchain."

"Now, imagine three days go by. The seller finally realizes they've been scammed and tries to sound the alarm. Even if they complain to the community, there's nothing anyone can do—the transaction is irreversible. When people hear that a double-spending attack has happened, they panic. They dump their Bitcoin out of fear, and the price crashes."

"And sure, you've 'successfully' double-spent the Bitcoin, but now the whole market knows what you've done. Investigators like *ZachXBT* track your transactions, and every crypto exchange and service provider is on alert, ready to freeze your funds the moment you try to cash out. Your reputation is ruined, and you can't even move the stolen Bitcoin without risking getting caught. So, while it may look like you pulled off a successful double-spend, the reality is you've wasted all that effort."

Bob leaned in, trying to make things clearer. "That said, while it might seem possible for miners to attempt a double spend, the reality is quite different. Yes, they create new blocks, and in theory, they could try to mess with the system. But in practice, it's really not worth it for them."

"Think about it," he continued. "If a miner wanted to pull that off, they would need to outpace the entire network. Essentially, this means they would need to create new blocks faster than all the other miners which means using massive amounts of electricity and computing power. And if they're going through all that trouble, they would probably aim for a big transaction, not something small. Why risk their reputation and resources for a tiny gain, right?"

"Even then," Bob added, "the consequences would be huge. The Bitcoin network is designed to make it extremely difficult to pull off any double-spending, let alone something big like that. If a miner did manage it, the news would spread fast, and it would cause chaos.

The community would lose trust, and the price of Bitcoin would likely crash."

"So, these miners who've spent a fortune collecting Bitcoin could end up holding something worth a lot less than they paid for it. It's like shooting themselves in the foot. In the end, they've got too much at stake to risk it all on a scheme that would backfire spectacularly. Most miners understand that being honest is way more profitable in the long run than trying to pull a fast one. So yeah, the risk is out there, but it's not something that will likely happens in my opinion."

Alice still looked puzzled and said, "I mean, if the network will catch that eventually, what's the big deal then? I can't help but feel that Satoshi was trying to solve a problem that didn't really exist."

Bob chuckled, "You know, your question actually proves that Bitcoin has nailed the double spending problem that was a concern identified by Satoshi right from the start. It's a big deal if you think about how Bitcoin works today. The whole system is designed to prevent double spending. Picture a scenario where a digital money—let's say it's not Bitcoin—functions like cash but lacks safeguards against double spending. Now, imagine yourself as a shop owner, and I stroll in wanting to buy something with this digital money. I could easily double spend, leaving you without your product and without any payment. That puts sellers in a tough spot—they can't afford to lose inventory without getting paid."

"So, the very fact that you're asking if double spending is even a real problem shows just how much progress Bitcoin has made. It's like the system is so effective at preventing it that it feels like a non-issue to you. That really speaks to how well it's working. Agree?"

Alice interrupted with a sharp, "Wait." She looked at Bob intently, sensing that he was giving Bitcoin too much credit. "I don't think that's entirely true," she continued. "If double spending is still a possibility, no matter how unlikely, doesn't that mean Bitcoin hasn't actually 'solved' the problem? It sounds like what's really stopping people from double spending isn't some bulletproof technical safeguard, but more of a psychological or financial deterrent."

She paused to gather her thoughts, then explained further, "Think about it. The network doesn't immediately prevent someone from trying to double spend—it's still technically possible. What keeps people from attempting it is the risk and cost of failure. If someone tried to double spend, they would need the majority of the network's mining power, which is extremely expensive and impractical. So really, it's more about the economic disincentives and the risk of getting caught than Bitcoin eliminating the possibility altogether. Do you not think so?"

Bob smiled, seeing the conversation deepening. "I get your point, Alice, but I think it's crucial to understand that the psychological deterrent against double spending is actually rooted in Bitcoin's design."

"Consider the psychological hurdle you face when you realize you have to put in a lot of money upfront to attempt a double spending operation. That hefty investment definitely makes you think twice before even considering double spending. Interestingly, this mental barrier is actually tied to how Bitcoin's proof of work mining is set up. Mining requires a tremendous amount of energy and resources, making any attempt to take control of the network incredibly expensive. Without this expensive framework in place, that psychological barrier would just vanish. Right?"

"Now, when you realize that anyone can easily spot your actions, it definitely makes you pause and reconsider any thoughts of trying to double spend. Plus, to pull off a double spend, you would need to take control of the majority of the mining power. While that might seem possible, there's a real worry that the community will catch on to your intentions. Staying under the radar is incredibly tough. Why is that? It's because Bitcoin operates without a central authority, meaning no single person or organization can manipulate the system. The community actively watches over the network to ensure that no one gains too much power. If one miner tries to dominate, the rest of the community will swiftly step in to defend the network. This setup makes it extremely difficult for anyone to successfully double spend. And here's the kicker: every Bitcoin transaction is like having millions of witnesses. See what I am saying? The psychological barrier we're discussing here really stems from Bitcoin's transparent and decentralized design."

"Next, the thought that if you try to double spend, you're really just shooting yourself in the foot, making you rethink any plans to cheat the system. Why is that? Because you're incentivized by Bitcoin itself. When you become a miner, you're not just part of the network; you have a vested interest in its success. Every time you mine, you're working to earn Bitcoin, and any attempt to double spend undermines the very system that rewards you. If the network were to suffer due to your actions, the value of your own earnings would plummet. It's like being on a team—if you sabotage the team, you're ultimately harming yourself. Once again, this mental barrier is largely a result of Bitcoin's design."

"Then, to attempt a double spend, you would have to be certain that your fraudulent transaction wouldn't be the one picked up by other miners and added to the blockchain—otherwise, your whole plan could come crashing down. But even if you somehow managed to control a majority of the mining power, nothing is guaranteed. Just that concern alone is enough to make you rethink any shady intentions. And why does that matter? Because you understand that Bitcoin transactions are irreversible, and every transaction must go through a thorough verification process."

"So, Alice, here is the bottom line: if you're suggesting that the only thing preventing double spending is some psychological factors rather than the actual design of Bitcoin, I would counter argue that this psychological barrier actually stems entirely from how Bitcoin is structured. While it might seem like double spending could happen, the way Bitcoin is built gives people plenty of compelling reasons to stick to the rules and act honestly."

He continued, "That being said, I'm not saying Bitcoin is flawless. These days it's nearly impossible to pull off double spending, but back in the early days, when there were only a handful of miners, and people were still figuring things out, I am guessing it could be a lot easier. Even so, Bitcoin's price was so low back then that if anyone tried double spending, it was probably just to mess around and test things out, not to actually make money off it."

Bob gave Alice a wink, and she took a moment to process what he had said.

Alice replied. "That's definitely an interesting way to look at it. But Bob, speaking of the delay... I mean that 10 minutes block time, I get how it can have its perks, depending on the situation. But if I wanted to send Bitcoin to a friend, it would really take at least ten minutes for them to receive it?"

She shook her head slightly. "For something that's supposed to be revolutionary and digital, ten minutes feels... underwhelming. I know there's the *Lightning Network* for faster payments, but it's not like everyone's using that yet, right? With all the hype around Bitcoin, I thought even the regular transactions would be quicker by now. I guess I expected it to be more streamlined—at least on par with the speed of apps we use every day. Ten minutes? It doesn't feel like the leap forward everyone claims it to be, not when we're used to instant transfers."

Bob smiled sympathetically. "I get why that sounds frustrating," he said. "It's true that there are some newer crypto projects out there that claim to achieve speed, decentralization, and security all at once. But I think it's equally important to remember that Bitcoin was the first of its kind. Satoshi was working with the technology available at the time, and he had to prioritize certain principles over others."

He shrugged slightly. "So yeah, Bitcoin was supposed to be *electronic cash*, which makes you wonder why speed didn't seem that important to Satoshi back then. If the idea was to create a currency for everyday use, you would of course think fast processing times would be a big deal, right? And, since the delay is kind of built into the system on purpose, I'm not even sure Satoshi saw 'speed' as the main goal at all. It seems like the system is designed more for security and decentralization than for speed."

"Maybe he didn't think about speed as much as he should have, assuming things would just get better as the network grew. Or maybe he realized that speed, decentralization, and security don't always play nice together,[12] so he chose to focus on building trust through security and decentralization instead. After all, if people are going to use a revolutionary type of currency, they need to feel confident that their transactions are safe and that the whole system is reliable. Strong security helps establish that trust, making it more likely that users will adopt Bitcoin for their daily purchases."

"But again, if Bitcoin was intended to be used as electronic cash, then transaction times definitely should have been a consideration. After all, if people get frustrated waiting for transactions to be confirmed, they might hesitate to use it for everyday purchases. I don't know; I guess nothing is perfect. Let's be honest—Satoshi might not have anticipated that the issue of speed would spark such a heated debate today."

Alice listened intently as Bob explained his points, her brow furrowed in thought. She nodded along, processing the complexities of Bitcoin's design and the unexpected challenges it faced.

Bob resumed. "And Alice, I hate to break it to you, but transactions can actually take even longer than 10 minutes, especially when the network is packed with transactions. But here's a little secret: if you're willing to pay higher fees, you can actually jump the queue. Miners prioritize transactions with higher fees, so paying more can get your transaction processed faster, even during busy times."

Alice's frown deepened as she folded her arms. "So, it's like waiting in line at a concert, where each block is a show with limited seats. If the line's too long, people have to wait for the next one. But

---

[12] Read Ethereum co-founder, Vitalik Buterin's *The Blockchain Trilemma*.

if you pay extra, you get a VIP pass and skip ahead, while everyone else is stuck waiting. That feels unfair—like the whole system favors those who can afford to pay more. Isn't that just like tipping? You're paying extra to get better service. But why should I have to pay more just to speed things up? No, actually, it's worse than tipping—it feels more like extortion. If you don't cough up the fee, they're basically saying they will consider not processing your transaction at all. It feels like a threat!"

Bob raised an eyebrow and leaned in. "I get how it can seem unfair at first, but that's exactly how the fee market competition works. Miners are going to prioritize transactions that pay higher fees because, at the end of the day, they have costs to cover. It's not just about volunteering their time; there's real money going into keeping those machines running. So, if you want your transaction confirmed quickly, you have to pay enough to make it worth their while. Otherwise, you risk getting stuck at the back of the line. If you want your transaction to get processed, you just have to play by the rules. But tell me, Alice, would you be happy working without getting paid?"

Alice raised an eyebrow, contemplating his question. "Well, they get new Bitcoin as a reward for their work, right? So, in a way, they're still earning something. What would happen if this fee wasn't part of the incentive system from the start? Wouldn't that change everything?"

Bob nodded, a thoughtful look on his face. "You know, I think Satoshi set up the fee structure to make sure miners have a good reason to include all transactions.[13] Especially for those smaller ones that might get overlooked. Sure, they earn new Bitcoin as a reward for their work, but that's just part of the picture. The fees really give them that extra nudge to include every single transaction."

He chuckled and added, "It's almost like Satoshi designed it to take advantage of the penny-pinching side of miners. You know,

---

[13] Cryptography Mailing List. Satoshi Nakamoto's reply to James A. Donald. Subject: Bitcoin P2P e-cash paper. November 10, 2008 at 22:18:20 UTC

giving them that extra incentive to scoop up those small transactions just to make sure they don't miss out on a little extra cash."

The gentle hum of conversation in the Tokyo café was occasionally interrupted by an animated exchange at a nearby table. Bob glanced over, intrigued by a middle-aged man gesturing excitedly toward a small ceramic pot. The pale green powder he was pointing at—matcha tea—caught Bob's attention. The man's fervent but hardly audible voice carried an intensity that suggested a deep conviction.

Alice followed Bob's gaze, curiosity flickering across her face. "What's going on over there?" she whispered, trying to catch a glimpse.

Bob leaned in, intrigued himself. "Looks like they're debating matcha. The man's all about whisking it by hand with a bamboo whisk—the traditional way. It's how they dissolve the matcha powder into the water to create that smooth, frothy texture you see in a proper bowl of matcha tea."

Alice raised an eyebrow, interested. "And what's the other person saying?"

Bob grinned, clearly amused by the dynamic. "She's pushing for the electric whisk—faster, easier, and still gets the froth. It's a debate between slow, methodical effort and modern efficiency. Actually," he added with a chuckle, "it reminds me of a similar debate in the crypto world."

Alice's interest was clearly piqued. "Oh? How so?"

Bob smiled, ready to draw the parallel. "In the world of cryptocurrencies, there's a similar kind of debate. Proof of Work, like using the traditional bamboo whisk, takes dedication and a steady approach—it's precise and requires a fair amount of energy. Then there's *Proof of Stake*, which is like using an electric whisk—it gets the job done with less effort and more efficiency."

"So, what exactly is Proof-of-Stake?" Alice probed.

Bob leaned back, ready to explain. "Here's the basic idea: Both Proof of Work and Proof of Stake are essentially mechanisms to ensure crypto transactions get added to the digital ledger in an orderly, truthful, and unchangeable way. If you want to add something to that ledger, you have to prove your good intentions—mostly by investing your hard-earned money in the system. That way, you're less likely to cheat or sabotage the system because you're putting your money where your mouth is. And when you do your job honestly, you're rewarded."

He leaned in slightly, keeping the comparison simple. "Both systems require you to invest, but the approach is quite different. With Proof of Work, you're buying and running costly mining hardware that not only drains electricity but also racks up those hefty power bills month after month. It's not just a one-time expense. On the other hand, Proof of Stake asks you to lock up a certain amount of your money, typically in the project's own cryptocurrency. And if you don't play by the rules, you risk losing some of that money."

Bob smiled as he continued, "In Proof of Work, you're known as a *miner*. In Proof of Stake, you're a *validator*. I sometimes think of miners as independent contractors—constantly competing against each other to win the next job, always hustling to stay ahead. Validators, on the other hand, are more like stakeholders, working to protect the system and ensure its success, all while earning rewards in return."

Alice tapped her chin thoughtfully, her eyes narrowing as she mulled over Bob's analogy. "So, validators kind of get paid for playing it smart—once they've shown their commitment, they just need to keep things steady. But miners? They're constantly in a race, always proving themselves again and again. It's like miners are the *work-hard* version, and validators are the *work-smart* version." She grinned, clearly pleased with her comparison.

Bob chuckled softly, trying to strike a balance. "I wouldn't want to say validators aren't working hard—it's just a different kind of effort. They still requires commitment and responsibility, but yes, the workload is a bit different. They lock up their stake and follow the rules to keep the network secure, but they don't have to constantly run expensive hardware or burn through energy like miners do. That's why it can naturally feel more like 'working smart.'"

"And let's not discount the miners. They play a critical role in the Proof of Work system. One of the advantages of it is its robust security. Miners invest in expensive hardware and face sky-high electricity bills that can be staggering—think thousands of dollars a month. Mind you this ongoing cost isn't just a one-time investment; it's a continuous commitment that can quickly add up. These high operational costs create a significant barrier to entry for anyone considering a malicious attack on the network. After all, who would want to risk blowing through a fortune just to try and cheat the system? The steep bills act as a deterrent, ensuring that only serious players with a real stake in the network participate."

As their conversation wound down, Bob subtly nodded toward the nearby table, where the middle-aged man and the lady were still deep in their animated debate about matcha.

Alice smirked slightly, her eyes twinkling with curiosity. "So, Bob, are you secretly rooting for the lady's side here? Do you prefer Proof of Stake, like her electric whisk, over Proof of Work's more 'hands-on' approach?"

Bob chuckled, shaking his head lightly. "Oh, no picking sides that easily," he replied with a grin. "Both have their ups and downs."

Alice leaned in, eyes curious. "So, tell me, which cryptocurrencies are using Proof of Work and which ones are using Proof of Stake?"

Bob leaned back, thinking for a moment. "Bitcoin's the big one for Proof of Work. Have you heard of *Litecoin* and *Dogecoin*? They use it too—they're like Bitcoin's smaller cousins, working the same way with all that computational power. Then you've got Ethereum, which started out with Proof of Work but recently switched to Proof of Stake with Ethereum 2.0."

"Just a heads-up, Alice," he said, leaning forward slightly. "Don't fall into the trap of thinking a crypto project fits neatly into one category, like strictly Proof of Work or Proof of Stake. Nowadays, almost every innovative project has its own unique mechanism, blending elements from various systems to meet their specific goals."

He continued, "There's always room for customization. Developers can apply different sets of rules to different aspects of the project, depending on what they need to balance—whether it's security, speed, or decentralization. So, it's not always black and white, and sometimes they mix and match."

Alice drummed her fingers lightly on the edge of the table, her lips curling into a teasing grin. "You know, Bob," she said with a hint of amusement, "every time we dive into this, it feels like we're in a two-man fan club for Bitcoin and Ethereum. Are those the only ones you're rooting for, or just the loudest voices in the room?"

Bob laughed, shaking his head. "Not even close," he replied. "Bitcoin and Ethereum are definitely the giants, but there's a whole world beyond them. Take *Cardano*, for instance—they take pride in their peer-review process, which seems similar to academic publishing. Then there's *Polkadot*, which focuses on connecting different blockchains and enabling them to work together."

Alice's drumming stopped, her interest piqued. Bob leaned in a bit, continuing, "*Avalanche* claims its transactions are finalized in less than one second—super fast, right? *BNB* started with Binance, the largest centralized crypto exchange in the world, but it has evolved into its own distinct entity. And then there's *Dogecoin*—yeah, the meme coin that started as a joke but is still holding its own. *XRP Ledger* is built for businesses, while *Hedera* boasts an impressive list of *tenured* governing council members, including IBM, Google, Deutsche Telekom, and Nomura. Lastly, you have projects dedicated to crypto finance, like *Uniswap*, *1inch*, *Curve*, and *PancakeSwap*."

"And honestly, there are tons of other fascinating projects out there, each with its own quirks and ambitions. I wish I could dive into all of them, but there's just not enough time! The innovation happening in the crypto world is wild—every project seems to add its own spin to the mix."

As Bob leaned back in his chair, he noticed Alice reaching for a napkin that had been resting beside her drink. The napkin was already covered in notes and doodles. Bob quickly realized these notes must have been made while he was up buying her an Americano earlier.

With a raised eyebrow and a chuckle, Bob commented, "Looks like you've been hard at work already. I see my little crypto list has made its way onto your napkin."

Alice glanced up, a spark of determination in her eyes. "Well, you mentioned all these intriguing projects, and I didn't want to forget them. This napkin is becoming quite the treasure trove of info!"

Bob's smile wavered as he watched Alice scribble furiously on the napkin. It suddenly struck him that she might be interpreting his list of crypto projects as some kind of recommendation. His playful demeanor shifted to a more serious tone.

He quickly raised his hands in mock defense. "Hold on, hold on, before you think I'm giving investment advice—*disclaimer* time!" He leaned in, eyes wide with exaggerated seriousness. "Just because I mentioned those projects, doesn't mean I'm recommending them. I'm not saying, 'Hey Alice, go buy some Dogecoin and Cardano tomorrow.'"

Alice chuckled, shaking her head. "So no insider tips from the crypto guru, huh?"

"Nope," Bob shot back, still grinning. "Just giving you a tour of the landscape. You've got to do your own homework, just like I do. Every project has its pros, cons, and quirks—and some are a lot riskier than others."

Alice's eyes sparkled with mischief as she leaned in, her voice playful. "So, you're saying I should be wary of your favorites?" she teased, clearly enjoying the back-and-forth.

Bob shrugged, laughing softly. "Okay, I'll admit—I can be a little biased, of course." He leaned back, crossing his arms with a playful grin. "You know, everyone's got their favorites, even if we try to stay neutral."

Alice tilted her head, teasing. "So, what's your bias then? Spill."

He smirked, tapping the side of his temple. "Ah, now that would be telling. But seriously, it's hard not to have a soft spot for certain projects when you've been in the space for a while. Doesn't mean I'm right, though. Just means I've spent way too many nights reading about them."

Alice rolled her eyes, smiling. "Of course, always the humble crypto guide."

As she continued to furiously wrote down key points, a frown of concentration creased her brow and her tongue peeked out in a classic sign of deep focus. Bob watched her with amusement, a playful glint in his eyes. It wasn't just the intensity of her concentration that caught his attention, but the way she meticulously crafted each word on the napkin.

"You know, for someone who claims not to be tech-savvy, your handwriting is surprisingly neat." Bob chuckled, leaning forward slightly.

Alice, startled from her concentration, looked up with a blush creeping across her cheeks. "Oh! I, uh, thanks," she stammered, self-consciously folding the napkin in half.

"It's just a habit from all those finance lectures. Gotta capture the key points somehow, right? Though, I can't say we ever went super deep into blockchain or crypto. Maybe it was mentioned briefly, but to be honest, back then I was probably more focused on acing those pesky exams."

Bob's grin widened. "Absolutely. And hey, no shame in using a napkin as a makeshift notepad. Necessity is the mother of invention, as they say."

Bob nodded with a smile. "The field is moving fast, and finance curriculums can take a while to catch up. But hey, your finance background is a great foundation! Understanding value, markets, and risk – all that stuff is crucial for crypto too."

A smile spread across Alice's face. She unfolded the napkin again, a newfound confidence in her eyes. Here she was, a finance major taking notes on cryptocurrencies on a napkin, but she was learning, and that was all that mattered. Bob's encouraging words had given her a boost.

Just as Alice was about to formulate her next inquiry, Bob's phone vibrated on the table. He glanced at the screen, his expression shifting slightly. "Oh, hold on a sec, Alice," he said, reaching for his phone. "This is my work."

He excused himself and stepped outside the café, his voice muffled through the glass doors as he spoke into the phone. Alice watched him, a brief moment of disappointment flickering across her face. She was eager to delve deeper into the world of Bitcoin, to explore the controversies surrounding it, and understand its potential impact on the future of finance.

With a sigh, Alice glanced down at her iced Americano. A thin, watery film shimmered on the surface, a stark contrast to the deep, rich espresso color it should have been. Disappointment flashed across her face. This wasn't the refreshing pick-me-up she had been craving anymore. She lifted the glass, the ice clinking softly against the sides. Taking a tentative sip, she confirmed her suspicions. The coffee was weak, the bold flavor of the espresso barely a whisper against the overwhelming dilution. A small frown played on her lips. Maybe, she thought, she could add another shot of espresso or a touch of simple syrup to salvage the drink.

Picking up her phone, she scrolled through social media feeds, the world of centralized finance and traditional currencies momentarily taking over her attention. As she flicked through images of crowded bank branches and headlines about government bailouts, the stark contrast to the decentralized nature of cryptocurrencies struck her even more.

Bob's return interrupted her digital sojourn. He slid back into his seat, a hint of apology in his eyes. "Sorry for that, Alice. Work emergency," he explained, tucking away his phone.

Alice, ever the curious soul, couldn't hide her eagerness. Her voice taking on a more strategic tone, "Bob, what if a whole bunch of people decided to get together and mess with the ledger? Like a group of hackers or something. Couldn't they overpower the system and change things?"

"That's a very astute observation, Alice," he admitted. "The truth is, no system is perfect. There is a potential vulnerability called a *51% attack*."

"A 51% attack?" Alice repeated, intrigued.

"Yes," Bob continued. "Imagine the consensus mechanism as a giant scale. If a single entity or group can control more than half of the computing power on the network – 51% or more – they could potentially disrupt the validation process. They could try to add invalid blocks, interfere legitimate transactions, or even rewrite past transactions."

"Wow, that sounds serious," Alice said, her voice laced with concern.

"It is," Bob agreed. "That's why the security of a blockchain really depends on how spread out it is. The more computers and people involved in the network, the tougher it is for any one group to take control. Sure, there are challenges, but the cool thing about blockchain is that it's always getting better and evolving. But even with all that, blockchain isn't completely foolproof. No system is, and I'm not about to defend it like it is."

Challenges

The conversation had been going on for hours. As Alice absorbed the details, she watched people passing by, reflecting on the contrast between the seemingly orderly world of traditional finance and the seemingly chaotic, yet promising world of cryptocurrencies. Her mind began to race with both excitement and apprehension. She was particularly intrigued by the ideals of decentralization, but certain concerns began to surface.

She looked up with a thoughtful expression. "Bob," she said, her tone shifting as she gathered her thoughts, "I get the appeal of decentralization, but I can't help but worry about some potential pitfalls."

"Shoot," Bob encouraged, leaning forward with a curious smile.

Alice took a deep breath, her gaze fixed on the busy street outside. "One big issue I see is *confirmation bias*," she began. "Think about online communities. People tend to surround themselves with others who agree with them, filtering out anything different. This creates echo chambers where everyone just hears the same message, reinforcing their existing beliefs. How can you have a well-rounded discussion or make good decisions if everyone's stuck in their own bubble? Similarly, with decentralization, there's a risk of creating isolated information silos. People never encounter arguments that challenge their assumptions, leading to a distorted view of reality. This can have serious consequences. Imagine a decentralized project making a critical decision based on flawed information simply because everyone in the echo chamber believed it to be true. Decentralization, while intended to empower individuals, could inadvertently create a breeding ground for misinformation and bad decisions."

Bob listened intently. "That's a compelling argument," he admitted. "Confirmation bias is definitely possible, but doesn't the freedom of decentralization help counteract that? People have the option to explore different communities and perspectives, don't they?"

"Maybe," Alice conceded. "But it appears to me that in a decentralized world, the onus falls entirely on the individual to break free from their echo chamber. And let's be honest, Bob, how many people are willing to put in that extra effort, especially when surrounded by the comforting din of agreement?"

She continued, her voice gaining conviction. "And what about leadership in this decentralized world? In traditional systems, leaders emerge because of their experience or knowledge. But with no central authority in crypto, who's in charge? What if a charismatic individual with a strong personality, but not necessarily the best ideas, starts swaying the crowd?"

"So, you're worried about a decentralized cult of personality forming?" Bob clarified.

Alice grinned. "Maybe not a cult, but there's a potential for power imbalances. Imagine someone with a lot of resources, who's a master at online persuasion, constantly pushing their proposals. Even if their ideas are flawed, they might hold more weight simply because they're louder and more visible. And then there's the issue of decision-making itself. Everyone has an opinion, but most probably lack the expertise to make a thoroughly evaluated decision. How long will it take for a large, decentralized group, potentially millions of people, to reach an agreement on anything? It could be a slow, cumbersome process, right?"

Bob leaned back in his chair. "Like a room full of people trying to perform brain surgery? "

Alice burst out laughing. "Exactly! Decentralization sounds great in theory – everyone has a say – but in reality, wouldn't it be like a giant playground with no rules? Everyone's running around with their own ideas, and chaos ensues."

Bob stroked his chin thoughtfully. "You're painting a vivid picture, Alice. But here's the thing: Just like playgrounds need rules to keep things fair and safe, different cryptocurrencies have their own set of unique rules to make sure that every transaction is legit and can be trusted. It's like a digital playground where everyone plays by the same rules and nobody's trying to pull a fast one."

Alice's eyes widened with newfound interest. "Rules? Now that sounds interesting. Tell me more, please."

"Sure, but before that," Bob said, "Why don't we start by looking at your concerns about decentralization from a few different angles? First up, confirmation bias. You're right, it's a real issue – but is it a decentralization problem? Think about it – centralized platforms can curate content and censor opposing viewpoints. Decentralization, with its lack of central authority, actually promotes exposure to diverse perspectives. Anyone can publish their ideas, and the community decides which ones hold weight."

He continued. "Now, the rise of influential figures within these communities. It's true, some individuals might gain influence because of their technical expertise or resources. But here's the key: their power isn't absolute. The community can still evaluate their proposals, and if those proposals don't resonate, they won't be implemented."

"So, it's a kind of meritocracy within the decentralized space?" Alice asked.

"You could see it that way," Bob admitted. "In a decentralized system, individuals who consistently contribute valuable insights, work, or innovations can naturally gain influence and respect within the community. Their leadership is earned through demonstrated ability rather than formal appointments by a handful of executives. They need to offer something valuable to the community, an idea that resonates. If their proposals aren't good, the community will reject them. It's not an echo chamber, Alice. It's a constant conversation. Moreover, if a leader's ideas go sour down the road, the community can choose to ignore them or even *fork* the project –

create a whole new one based on different principles. That's the beauty of decentralization – freedom of choice and action."

"True, but what if the conversation gets bogged down?" Alice countered. "Decision-making with a large, decentralized group sounds slow and cumbersome. How long could it take to agree on something?"

Bob acknowledged, "Slowness can be frustrating, that's true. But remember, while decisions might not be instantaneous, but they aren't endless either. These communities often set deadlines. It's not like endless debates. Slow and deliberate decision-making can sometimes be a good thing. It allows for thorough vetting of proposals and identification of potential flaws. Imagine a centralized authority rushing through a decision that ends up having disastrous consequences. Besides, if a deadline needs to be extended, it's because a major flaw has been identified. It's all about getting things right, not rushing blindly."

She paused, her eyes narrowing as a new concern crossed her mind. "So, maybe slowness isn't all bad..." Her expression shifted, and she leaned forward slightly, her tone more urgent this time. "Wait, but what about emergencies? What if a critical decision needs to be made quickly, like in the case of a security breach?"

"There are usually contingency plans in place for those situations," Bob explained. "The community can also delegate certain decisions to smaller groups for faster action, as long as it adheres to the overall project goals."

"And lastly," Bob continued, "you mentioned people lacking expertise for informed decisions. This assumes centralized authorities always make perfect decisions. History is littered with examples of the opposite, Alice. The 2008 financial crisis, a period of severe economic downturn, is often cited as an example of potential shortcomings in centralized decision-making. Imagine life and death in the hands of just a dozen individuals. Decentralization, despite its imperfections, offers a system where a wider range of voices can be heard and potentially prevent similar isolated decision-making. While it may be messy at times, it can serve as a valuable tool for preventing similar centralized mistakes."

Bob leaned back, his tone more skeptical. "That being said, Alice, the way people throw around the term 'decentralization' is pretty misleading. They talk like these crypto projects just pop into existence and run on their own, but that's so far from the truth. I mean, who starts these projects? Who's running the day-to-day stuff—fixing bugs, handling marketing, building the website, making key decisions? It's not some autonomous system—it's a team of people, and in most cases, that means the project is centralized, at least in how it operates."

He continued. "Sure, they might say it's 'decentralized' because they use blockchain, but when you look closer, there's usually a group of individuals pulling the strings, making the big calls. So when people brag about 'decentralization,' what they really should be focusing on is how the community is empowered to some extent, like having a louder voice in certain decisions. But even that doesn't mean all voices are equal. If you don't like what the project is doing, you can always leave—that's probably the biggest freedom you get."

"To me, 'decentralization' has always been a *spectrum*, not some on-off switch. Most of these projects are far more centralized than they let on. It's just smart to be critical and see it for what it really is, rather than buying into the hype."

Alice asked, "Even Bitcoin?"

Bob sighed, nodding slightly. "Yeah, even Bitcoin. Bitcoin might not have a central entity calling the shots on decisions, but what good is that when just a few whales can move the price around? It's still open to manipulation, just in a different way. It's like saying a game is fair just because there are no official referees, but a handful of players still have all the cards. Decentralized? Sure, technically. But not as much as people like to believe."

Alice raised an eyebrow. "If the community is so into decentralization, why don't they speak out about these issues?"

Bob leaned back, thinking for a moment. "You know, it's probably a bit of a dilemma," he said. "When institutions start buying up and accumulating Bitcoin, it sends a signal to the rest of the world that Bitcoin isn't some worthless asset. I mean, if even these big institutions want a piece of it, it can't be all bad, right? So instead of tackling the hard truth about decentralization, a lot of folks would rather just go with the flow and hope the price goes up."

He shrugged, a gentle smile forming. "Don't get me wrong. It's not that anyone is being disingenuous. A lot of people genuinely care about decentralization and want to see it thrive. The truth is, there are voices out there raising concerns, but it can be tough to change the narrative when the momentum is so strong. Wanting to profit from Bitcoin is perfectly natural; we all do. But I can't shake the feeling that it's just a matter of time before those whales start dumping on everyone. The way some prominent Bitcoin holders shill it, combined with how the price keeps rising, it's a bit surreal. We've got to stay realistic about what decentralization really means and keep those conversations going."

Alice frowned, intrigued. "So what could happen after the whales decide to dump their holdings?"

Bob shrugged slightly. "Well, the market will probably panic, and we might see a pretty wild drop in prices. But honestly? I don't think Bitcoin will just disappear. It's too established for that. It could actually be a good thing, in a way. While I know many Bitcoiners believe today's price is already undervalued, and believe me, I get that perspective, but it could be an opportunity for the price to settle into a range that feels more sustainable to many people. Sometimes a reality check is what the market needs. If some current holders decide to walk away, it might create space for a new wave of 'Baby Boomers' in the Bitcoin world. These are the folks who thought they had missed the boat initially but are now ready to jump on and find themselves in a unique position. Who knows? They might just be the ones who truly benefit in the long run, seizing the opportunity when the price adjusts. It's all a bit unpredictable, but maybe that's just how it goes in the crypto world."

Bob's face lit up as he thought back to something fascinating he read in *Digital Gold* by *Nathaniel Popper*. He hadn't quite finished the book yet, but it had definitely grabbed his attention while he was at the café before Alice's matcha spill.

"You know, the first known Bitcoin-to-USD transaction was actually based on the rough cost of electricity needed to generate a coin," he said, leaning in.

"It's funny how Bitcoin might seem abstract to most people, but its creation is anything but. That first pricing tied to an electricity bill really drives home a key point: there's a real, tangible cost to creating Bitcoin—energy and computational power. It doesn't just appear out of thin air. Real work, and more importantly, real money, goes into bringing it into existence. Just like any product or service, Bitcoin comes with production costs, and someone bears that cost upfront."

With that, Bob gestured toward the book resting face down on the table. "By the way, I think this is a good read," he said, flipping it over to reveal the cover: *Digital Gold*.

As Alice picked up the book, she couldn't help but notice its unimpressive cover—a dull, almost single-color design with no graphics, just plain text. The title stood out in a large font, and beneath it, the subtitle *Bitcoin and the inside story of the misfits and millionaires trying to reinvent money*, caught her eye.

The book was thick, and as she flipped it open, the dense text and small fonts inside suggested a long, detailed read. It wasn't a light read for sure. Yet, despite the lackluster presentation, Alice found herself inexplicably drawn to it. Maybe it was the intrigue of the subtitle—misfits and millionaires—an unusual combination that promised more than just dry financial analysis. As she flipped through, the dense paragraphs felt packed with stories and information. The book felt substantial in the weight of its content. She could sense there were layers of history and drama behind Bitcoin's origin—something about it felt important, like it was offering a rare peek behind the curtain into a world she hadn't fully understood before. The more she skimmed, the more she wanted to dive in and uncover the tales hidden inside those small, unassuming fonts.

"This is actually fascinating," she murmured, almost to herself.

Bob watched her with a smile, clearly pleased that the book had captured her attention. "Yeah, it's more than just numbers on a screen," he said. "There's a whole backstory to how it started."

After a brief pause, she asked, "Speaking of mining, can I do it at home? Like, is it something I can just set up with my computer?"

Bob smiled. "Well, you could try, but it's not as simple as it used to be. Back in the early days of Bitcoin, people could mine with regular computers at home. But now, the competition is so high, and the puzzles are so complex, that you need specialized, powerful equipment to have any real chance. It's not really practical for most people to mine at home anymore unless you've got some serious hardware and are ready for high electricity costs."

"But if you're still interested, there's another option—you can join a mining *pool*. Basically, it's a group of people who pool their resources together to solve those puzzles. Instead of one person doing all the heavy lifting, everyone contributes a bit of their computing power, and when the pool earns Bitcoin, it's shared among everyone based on how much they contributed. I've got a habit of calling the operators of these mining pools *wholesale* miners—they're really the ones helping to keep the game going. It's a clever way for smaller, *retail* miners to still participate without needing all that expensive equipment."

Alice frowned slightly, thinking it over. "But wait, if 'retail' miners are joining forces in these mining pools, doesn't that create another problem? Couldn't those pools become so big that they start to control the network? Wouldn't that be a threat to decentralization?"

Bob smiled at her sharp insight. "You're right to think about that. Mining pools do have the potential to become large, and if one pool controlled more than 50% of the total computational power, it could potentially manipulate the network. It's something people in the crypto community are always watching out for."

Alice leaned in, curious. "Has that ever happened?"

Bob nodded slowly. "There have been times when a few mining pools have gotten close to controlling a majority of the network's power, but generally, the community reacts by decentralizing more, meaning 'retail' miners might leave large pools and join smaller ones. They usually don't want to see a single pool control too much power, because it would undermine the very system they're benefiting from."

"How would that affect the value?" Alice asked.

"Think about it this way," Bob explained. "If a few players control the network, they could alter transaction records or even attempt to double-spend Bitcoin, which would basically destroy the whole point of the system. When people lose trust in a currency or a financial system, its value plummet. No one would want to use it anymore."

"You would think that those 'wholesale' miners, with all their resources, might feel justified or entitled to exert control over the mining ecosystem, right? But here's the thing: they've invested a significant amount of money into their mining rigs, electricity, and all the other costs just to earn Bitcoin. They could manipulate the system, sure, but they would essentially be shooting themselves in the foot. Their hard-earned Bitcoin would likely plummet in value and could even become worthless. Psychologically, it's in their best interest to keep the system decentralized to maintain the value of what they've worked so hard to accumulate."

Bob chuckled, shaking his head. "Honestly, if I were one of them, I would be scared to death watching my pool approach 50% of the global mining power. I mean, sure, I would have the ability to exert control, but I wouldn't have any control over how the market would react to that. It's a risky game. The moment people start feeling uneasy about centralization, the trust in the whole system could evaporate. And if that happens, the value of my hard-earned Bitcoin could nosedive. It's a terrifying thought. The last thing I would want is to see the value of what I've built turn to dust just because I crossed that line."

Alice raised an eyebrow, leaning forward. "But that's assuming everyone has good intentions, right? What if someone starts a mining pool with the plan to centralize power and disrupt the whole system? They could just flip the script and try to bring Bitcoin down from the inside, like a plot to overthrow it."

Bob nodded slowly, considering her point. "That's definitely a possibility. But I can't help but wonder if it's really worth it. To set up a mining pool, you need to invest a ton of money upfront—equipment, electricity, all of it. It would have to be one insane but somehow workable plot to risk all that for something so destructive. I mean, why gamble your investment just to watch the whole thing crumble?"

Alice leaned in closer, her tone conspiratorial. "But think about it—what if someone has a bigger agenda? Picture a large financial institution, feeling threatened by the rise of Bitcoin as a decentralized alternative. They could secretly back a mining pool or even multiple pools with enough resources to centralize control. With that power, they could manipulate transaction records, causing confusion and undermining trust in the system. It's like a Trojan horse, hiding their true intentions while they work from the inside to dismantle it."

She paused for effect, then continued, "Or consider a government that views Bitcoin as a challenge to their monetary policy. They might create a mining pool with the intent to disrupt the network and spread fear to dissuade people from using it. They could trigger a panic sell-off, buying up Bitcoin at rock-bottom prices while everyone else is in a frenzy, then cashing in when the market stabilizes. These are sinister tactics, but in a world driven by power and profit, you never know what lengths some might go to."

Bob let out a hearty laugh, shaking his head. "Wow, Alice, you've got a real talent for this whole conspiracy theory thing! I mean, seriously, you're connecting dots like a pro. But you know what? You're actually onto something. Those with deep pockets and hidden agendas could totally pull off something like that. It's like a high-stakes chess game where the rules are always changing. So while it might sound a bit wild, I wouldn't brush it off entirely."

Then, a serious note creeping into his voice. "You know, it's interesting—just like in the traditional financial system, *trust* is really the weakest link in Bitcoin, too. If someone wanted to bring down Bitcoin, all they would need to do is attack that trust. Create doubt, spread misinformation, or manipulate the narrative. That's why it's almost inexcusable for the crypto community to not stay educated and informed. If people panic, that's when things start to crumble. It's crucial to understand how the system works so we can defend it against those kinds of attacks. Knowledge is power in this space."

As Bob excused himself and headed to the restroom, Alice took the chance to breathe and clear her mind. Then it hit her—she had a ramen reservation, and the time was sneaking up on her. She pulled out her phone, opened Google Maps, and was relieved to see the restaurant was just a quick walk away.

When Bob returned, she smiled up at him. "Hey, I've got to get going. It's almost time for my reservation," she said, casually packing up her stuff.

"Got it," Bob replied, gathering his things without missing a beat. They walked together toward the door, the conversation still lingering in the air like an easy breeze.

As they were about to step outside, Alice suddenly stopped, turning to Bob with a smile. "Hey, how about lunch tomorrow? My treat," she said, her tone light but her eyes showing clear interest. "I would love to pick your brain some more about all this crypto stuff."

Bob grinned, clearly pleased with the offer. "Lunch sounds great! Any ideas where you would like to go?"

Alice laughed softly, shaking her head. "You're the local expert. You choose."

Bob thought for a moment, then his eyes lit up. "I know just the place. How about we try this cozy little spot that does amazing udon? It's close by and perfect for a relaxed lunch."

"Perfect," Alice agreed, pulling out her phone to jot down the details as Bob shared the location with her.

With their plans set, they exchanged an easy goodbye. Alice walked off toward the Ramen place, already looking forward to tomorrow's lunch.

Part Three

The next day, the sky was clear, and the gentle hum of city life filled the air as Alice made her way to the udon spot Bob had suggested. She felt relaxed, the casual pace of the morning settling her mood. As she approached the restaurant, she saw Bob already waiting outside, leaning casually against the entrance, looking up from his phone just as she arrived.

"Right on time," Bob greeted with a smile, straightening up.

"Wouldn't want to keep you waiting," Alice joked, returning the smile.

They stepped inside the small, cozy restaurant together, the aroma of fresh broth and noodles filling the air. It had a warm, traditional Japanese feel, with wooden tables and soft lighting that made it feel tucked away from the rush of the city outside.

Bob waved to the waiter and, after exchanging a few words in fluent Japanese, led Alice to a quiet corner booth. "This place is great—kind of a hidden gem," Bob said, sliding into the booth. "I think you'll like it."

Alice took her seat, glancing at the menu. "It already smells amazing."

They chatted easily as they decided on their orders. Bob recommended a classic udon with tempura on the side, and Alice went with his suggestion. The food arrived quickly—steaming bowls of thick, chewy noodles in rich broth, with golden-crisp tempura neatly arranged on the side.

"This looks fantastic," Alice said, picking up her chopsticks.

They started their meal, the conversation flowing naturally, but without diving straight into heavy topics. It was more relaxed this time—small talk about the city, some travel stories, and little anecdotes from their lives in Tokyo.

Alice couldn't help but feel a sense of ease, and Bob seemed just as laid-back. It was nice, just enjoying lunch for what it was—a break from the intensity of their previous conversation.

After they finished eating, Bob leaned back, satisfied. "That hit the spot."

"It really did," Alice agreed, nodding as she sipped the last of her tea. "Thanks for the recommendation."

Bob smiled, "You still owe me those crypto questions, though."

Alice laughed. "Don't worry, I haven't forgotten."

They both stood up, ready to continue their day. "How about we find a café for dessert or coffee?" Bob suggested as they walked toward the door. "We can pick up where we left off yesterday."

"Sounds like a plan," Alice said, her curiosity about Bitcoin and crypto sparking again as they headed down the street together, looking for the perfect café to dive back into their discussion.

As they strolled through the lively streets, the warm afternoon sun cast a golden glow over everything. They chatted casually about Tokyo's quirks and hidden spots until they came across a quaint little café tucked away down a narrow alley. Its vintage sign creaked softly in the breeze, and through the large windows, they could see a handful of customers enjoying their coffee in quiet corners.

"This looks perfect," Bob said, gesturing toward the door.

Alice nodded in agreement, and they stepped inside, greeted by the rich scent of freshly brewed coffee and a soft jazz tune playing in the background. The café had a cozy, rustic charm—dark wooden tables, bookshelves lined with well-loved novels, and potted plants giving it a homely feel.

They picked a spot near the window, where the late afternoon light streamed in, bathing the table in a warm glow. Bob waved over a server, ordered two iced coffees, and leaned back in his chair, looking relaxed.

"So," Bob said with a grin as the coffees arrived, "ready to get back into the crypto rabbit hole?"

Alice smiled, taking a sip of her drink. "Definitely. But first, I just realized I never thanked you for taking the entire afternoon yesterday to explain everything to me. I appreciate it—really. I've learned so much."

Bob waved her off playfully. "Hey, no problem at all. I enjoyed it too. It's nice to talk to someone who's genuinely curious."

As they sipped their coffees, Alice leaned forward. "Okay, so, here's a basic question for you—what happens when all the Bitcoins are mined? I mean, what keeps the miners going after that?"

"Good question. So, after all 21 million Bitcoins are mined, miners won't be getting block rewards anymore. But, they'll still earn from transaction fees, which is another reason why fee system is so important. It's what keeps everything running even when the mining rewards dry up," Bob explained.

"But what if, eventually, the fees aren't enough to motivate them?" Alice asked.

"Well, that's the big unknown, isn't it?" Bob said, a thoughtful look crossing his face. "We've got decades before that happens, and it's hard to predict. But if the network is still widely used by then, the fees should be enough to keep miners in the game. Plus, there's always the chance that technology and how we use Bitcoin will evolve."

She hesitated for a second before continuing, making sure her disagreement didn't come off too strong. "I get where you're coming from, Bob, but I don't think that's entirely it. I mean, the way you're talking about it, it feels like you might be in a bit of denial about the risks. I mean, sure, miners will rely on transaction fees, but will that really be enough? What if people lose interest in Bitcoin or the transaction volume doesn't grow like everyone hopes?"

She continued. "I mean, I just think there's more to it. I guess I just don't think it's as simple as 'the system will figure itself out.' There's a lot more at stake, and sometimes it feels like people are just hoping everything will go smoothly because it's too complicated to think about the *what ifs*."

Bob smiled thoughtfully, taking a moment before responding. "I get it, Alice, I really do. But here's the thing—this whole system, it's not like Satoshi overlooked any of this. It was intentional. The way Bitcoin's designed, with the last minting in 2140, it's built for the long haul. That's over a hundred years from now, and by then, the entire landscape—technology, economics, everything—could be completely different."

"Maybe Satoshi just got lucky, but honestly, that long timeline might've been exactly what Bitcoin needed to really thrive. What if, at some point, the price stabilizes, and we start seeing it actually being used as a global currency in some places? Governments are even getting in on the action, working together to run miner nodes and keep the whole system going. And maybe at this point, it's not really about the mining rewards anymore. What's keeping them motivated is the stability, security, and overall convenience of the system—it's become way bigger than just the reward for mining."

He paused, considering the idea further. "And maybe, just maybe, Satoshi had some kind of prediction for 2140—like a big war that could wipe out the entire world, rendering any form of money obsolete, even Bitcoin. If that's the case, it actually makes sense why he set the timeline for the last Bitcoin to be minted by then. With no global economy left to support it, there wouldn't be any need for new Bitcoins. It's almost as if Satoshi, with his mythical identity, could be seen as a time traveler. It's wild to think about, but anything is possible."

"Of course," Bob added with a smirk, "there's also the possibility that Satoshi simply didn't give it enough thought. I mean, even the so-called economists struggle to understand the economy half the time—predicting market dynamics is like trying to predict the weather. If they're still trying to figure it out, then expecting Satoshi to have planned for every twist and turn might be giving him a bit too much credit. I mean, who's to say he wasn't just putting something out there and leaving it up to the rest of us to figure out? Sometimes even the most genius ideas have gaps."

He shrugged, a small smile on his face. "It's all speculation, of course. Look, I'm not saying Satoshi had every answer mapped out from the start. Nobody could have predicted how far Bitcoin would come or where it'll go next. It's probably less about having a perfect blueprint and more about adapting to whatever comes."

Then, his eyes lit up with excitement as he leaned in, lowering his voice like he was letting Alice in on some grand, extraordinary conspiracy. "Think about it, our minds are basically just super advanced computers, right? So, what if by 2140, instead of a machine solving complex puzzles, it's people—using their own brainpower to keep the network running? Imagine by then we've developed neural interfaces that let people contribute brainpower, creativity, or even emotions to verify transactions or validate information. It's like turning mining into this mental challenge where everyone's part of the system, not just some code running in the background."

"And instead of getting Bitcoin as a reward, maybe it's access to some higher level of knowledge or experiences—stuff way beyond what we think of as money now. Our brains are pretty much the ultimate processors, so why not use them? In this world, we would be the new 'mining rigs,' plugging our thoughts right into the blockchain. Crazy, right?"

Alice raised an eyebrow, intrigued. "Wait, you're saying… we would use thoughts to mine Bitcoin?"

Bob nodded, eyes gleaming. "More than that, actually. How about the Bitcoin blockchain isn't just a ledger anymore? It's downloaded into everyone's minds, making each person a node in a vast, interconnected web of consciousness. People wouldn't just use the blockchain; they would *be* the blockchain itself. Each person would act like a live, breathing node, where instead of computers doing all the work, it's our brains processing and verifying information. So, everyone would be part of the system, contributing not just data but even their thoughts, emotions, or creativity, a real decentralized network that holds everything we know, feel, or experience. It would connect all of us in a huge web of shared consciousness, blurring the line between technology and the human mind. No central authority, no government, no computers, or traditional internet—just direct, raw exchanges of information, creating a seamless flow of transactions between human nodes transcending geographical boundaries."

Alice shook her head, a playful grin spreading across her face. "And by then, we might have to worry about people hacking into our minds and swiping our brainpower! Can you imagine? It's absolutely insane, but I love it. Who knows, maybe Bitcoin is paving the way for that! We could end up living in a world where our thoughts are the currency, and the only thing standing between us and some rogue hacker is a mental firewall."

She laughed, the thought sparking an adventurous thrill within her.

Bob's excitement took a sudden turn. His tone softened, his expression more serious now. "You know," he began, his voice quieter, "I really do think our brains are just... well, *computers*. When you break it down, the way we process thoughts, store memories, solve problems—it's all just electrical signals, like data running through a machine. And when you think about the complexity of it, it's hard not to see us as some kind of really sophisticated *robots*, perfectly designed to perform these remarkable tasks."

He paused for a moment, eyes drifting as if searching for the right words. "But then, if that's true, doesn't it make you wonder? If we're these complex machines, there's got to be a *creator* behind all this—someone who designed both the software and the hardware, so to speak. And when we design robots and develop AI, it feels like we're trying to play god—creating intelligence that can think, learn, and maybe even become smarter than us. It's like a robot trying to make other robots, all in an attempt to outsmart the very one who programmed it. It's a bit ridiculous when you think about it. It makes you wonder about our place in all this, doesn't it? Are we crossing a line that wasn't meant to be crossed? I can't shake the feeling that there's a way we're supposed to follow, a deeper truth that's more than just what we see around us, and a life that's bigger than just… this." He gestured around, indicating the cafe, the world outside, everything.

Alice blinked, clearly caught off guard by the sudden shift, the depth behind what he was saying. "Wow, I didn't expect that. You really believe in that, huh?" She reacted.

Bob nodded, a slight smile softening his features. "Yeah, it's like… in all this talk about Bitcoin and crazy tech, I sometimes feel the need to reconnect with something bigger. If it came down to it, I would trade all the Bitcoin in the world for that. I guess it's all about surrendering to something greater, turning away from the chaos we have created, and finding peace in that connection."

Alice shifted in her seat, considering his words. "I get what you mean, but I must admit I can't quite wrap my head around faith like that. I tend to see things through a different lens, you know, the *Darwin* kind of thing."

Bob quickly realized he had veered off topic. "Sorry if I got a bit carried away there," he said, a sheepish grin appearing on his face. "I didn't mean to go off on a tangent."

Alice chuckled softly. "No need to apologize! I actually find it fascinating how you connect Bitcoin with faith. It's an interesting angle to explore."

Bob looked surprised but pleased. "Really? I thought I was just rambling. You know, some people actually treat Bitcoin like a form of faith. To many, that's almost like a *cult* mentality."

Alice raised an eyebrow, intrigued. "Really? How do you mean?"

Community

"Well, you've got these Bitcoin *maximalists*, , or just *maxis*, as they're often called," Bob explained. "To them, Bitcoin *is* Bitcoin—the only thing that really matters. Some of them won't even call it a cryptocurrency, because they see it as something entirely beyond that label. They treat it almost like a financial gospel, and anything else—any other crypto—they view as a distraction or not worth their time."

Alice paused for a moment, her expression shifting. "Wait, so the crypto community isn't as united as I imagined? It's actually divided?"

Bob nodded. "Yeah, it can be pretty fragmented. There are various factions within the community, each with different philosophies and priorities. For example, you have the Ethereum community who believe in the power of smart contracts and decentralized applications. Then there are DeFi advocates who are all about decentralized finance, arguing that traditional financial systems can be replaced entirely. Each group has its own vision, but the maxis are particularly vocal about their belief that Bitcoin is the ultimate solution."

Alice raised an eyebrow, intrigued. "What do you think drives the Bitcoin maxis, then? I mean, why be so focused on just Bitcoin? What's their motivation?"

Bob leaned back, considering Alice's question. "I think it's a mix of things," he began. "For some, it's probably a belief in decentralization, the idea that Bitcoin is the purest form of it. Maybe they see it as the only way to break free from government control or centralized finance. For others, it could just be... comfort. Bitcoin's been around the longest, proven itself over time, so maybe they think everything else is just noise or risky."

He paused, then added, "And then there's probably a bit of tribalism too. Once you invest so much time, energy, and identity into something, it's hard to accept that other ideas could work just as well—or even better. When you're that invested in something, watching other projects or coins gain traction can feel like a threat— like it's splitting the market share. It's almost as if they think any success outside of Bitcoin somehow weakens its position, even though the whole space could grow together."

"Another reason some folks turn into Bitcoin maxis is because they've dabbled in *altcoins* and ended up losing a chunk of cash. Just to fill you in, *altcoins* are any cryptocurrencies that aren't Bitcoin. People often invest in them thinking they'll strike it rich, but a lot of them can be pretty volatile or even turn out to be scams. It's like they've been burned, and now they're convinced that outside of Bitcoin, everything else is just a bunch of *shitcoins*. They've had their fun, but now they're sticking with what they believe is the real deal."

"And then there's that whole '1BTC = 1BTC' idea they throw around. I doubt if there is even a sensible definition among them about what that means at all. It feels like they're just repeating a slogan without thinking it through. If the value of everything around Bitcoin changes— for example, if the cost of goods and services keeps rising or people stop believing in Bitcoin—what good is saying 'one Bitcoin is one Bitcoin'? It sounds more like a wishful thinking than a real understanding of how economics works. In the real world, value is always relative. Prices fluctuate, and what matters is what you can actually *do* with that Bitcoin, not just holding onto it like it's some eternal constant. It's almost like they want to ignore how markets work, as if holding Bitcoin somehow puts you outside of those realities. But the truth is, unless Bitcoin can exist in a world where people actually use it for more than just speculation, that slogan doesn't mean much. It's more like a comforting mantra than a real strategy."

Alice raised an eyebrow, her curiosity piqued. "But what if their '1 BTC = 1 BTC' argument is just... literally true? I mean, isn't it just a straightforward statement?"

Bob chuckled, shaking his head. "Why are we even questioning the obvious?" he replied, a playful tone in his voice. "It's like saying 'one apple is one apple.' Sure, it's true, but it doesn't really tell you anything useful. It doesn't account for the fact that an apple can be worth a lot more or a lot less depending on the market—like if it's in season or if people suddenly decide they prefer oranges."

He paused, frowning. "I sometimes feel like the maxis exhibit traits similar to Borderline Personality Disorder. They have this intense, almost obsessive loyalty to Bitcoin that can swing from extreme idealization to harsh devaluation of anything else. It's like they see Bitcoin as their savior, while everything else—altcoins, *stablecoins*, you name it—are nothing but worthless 'shitcoins.' And when you criticize Bitcoin or even suggest that there might be other valid options out there, their reactions can be explosive. It's like flipping a switch; one minute, they're passionate advocates, and the next, you would think you had just insulted their mother. This emotional volatility can be intense. They cling to Bitcoin as if their entire identity depends on it, and any challenge to that belief feels like a personal betrayal. It's a fascinating, if a bit unsettling, dynamic."

He continued with a wry smile creeping onto his face. "And, you would think they would at least be united among themselves, right? Loyal to the cause or whatever? But no—far from it. They're just as toxic toward each other as they are toward everyone else. Honestly, Alice, I wouldn't bat an eye if some of them ditched Bitcoin the moment they realized the whole Bitcoin agenda no longer serves their own interests. That's when things really get ugly. The second someone in their circle starts questioning the dogma or veering off the script, they'll tear them apart just as viciously. It's like a viper's nest, all coiled up and ready to strike the moment things stop aligning with their needs. And when they finally decide Bitcoin isn't convenient anymore? You can bet they'll be the first to throw Bitcoin under the bus without a hint of remorse. It's like a reality show where the contestants are all too eager to stab each other in the back for a shot at fame and fortune. And here's the real kicker: when they do make that switch, they'll probably be even more venomous towards Bitcoin than they ever were towards other cryptos. It's as if they feel the need to lash out at their former 'true love' just to rationalize their betrayal. To them, it's all just a game, and they'll jump ship faster than you can say 'decentralization.'"

Alice raised an eyebrow. "But wouldn't that be the same for the whole crypto community, not just the Bitcoin maxis? I mean, they're all in it for their own gain, right?"

Bob shook his head firmly. "No, no—it's not the same. Sure, there's competition and drama everywhere, but the level of toxicity with the Bitcoin maxis is on a whole other scale. They've built this fortress around their belief system, and anyone who so much as questions it gets labeled as an enemy, even if it's another Bitcoiner. It's like they take any disagreement as a personal attack on their identity. In the broader crypto space, you'll see arguments, but there's at least room for innovation and new ideas. With maxis, it's more rigid—they guard that belief like it's their religion. And when someone steps out of line? The claws come out."

Alice hesitated for a moment, then asked, "So... if I own Bitcoin, does that mean people will think I'm one of these maxis? I mean, it sounds like the moment you even touch Bitcoin, you get lumped in with that crowd." She frowned, clearly puzzled by the idea that just holding Bitcoin could link her to that level of intensity.

Bob shook his head. "Nah, it doesn't work like that. Just having Bitcoin doesn't slap a 'maxi' label on you. It's more about the mindset, the way you approach it. You can own Bitcoin and still appreciate other stuff in the crypto world. Maxis are just the loudest, most hardcore bunch. We like to pretend we're the 'reasonable' ones, you know, open to new ideas and all that. But hey, maybe we're just fooling ourselves, thinking we're any less stubborn than they are." He smirked, clearly poking fun at his own thinking."

Bob leaned back in his chair and said, "I remember reading something by *Nic Carter*[14] about those Bitcoin maxis. He brings up

---

[14] https://x.com/nic__carter/status/1666294372537606145

some interesting points that really gave me a fresh perspective on that whole group."

Alice furrowed her brow in confusion. "Wait, you mean Nick Carter from the *Backstreet Boys*?"

Bob chuckled and shook his head. "No, not him! I'm talking about Nic Carter, the crypto guy. Totally different person! Actually, I didn't expect you to know about the Backstreet Boys. I thought that was a bit before your time."

Alice grinned playfully. "Hey, good music is timeless! Can't help but appreciate a classic boy band."

Bob chuckled, shaking his head at the unexpected turn in their conversation. "You know, it's funny how we went from boy bands to Bitcoin, but it actually makes sense. Just like a music group, Bitcoin's success really is a team effort. Think about it: Bitcoin's success isn't really because of the maxis. It's the broader community outside of them that's keeping things moving. Maxis contribute more noise than anything else, and without the rest of the community, Bitcoin wouldn't be where it is today and I'm not sure they would want to admit that. They seem hell-bent on isolating themselves from the very ecosystem that's propped Bitcoin up all these years. They are like those people who cross a bridge and then set it on fire behind them, acting like they don't need anyone else to get where they're going. It's delusional, really."

"Let's be honest here: who are they to boast? Almost everyone in the space believes Bitcoin is the best option out there. The difference is that while many of us recognize its potential without the drama, the maxis take it to a whole new level, acting all high and mighty just for holding onto it. And let's face it, most of them are probably just clutching a tiny bag of it, yet they act as if they're the *guardians* of the entire crypto space. They might think they're part of some exclusive club, but really, it's just a case of sitting on their hands while the rest of the world moves forward."

Bob smirked, his voice dropping a bit as he leaned closer, almost conspiratorial. "Sometimes I even wonder if the whole maxi community isn't even real—or at least not as organic as they make it seem. I mean, it's almost too aggressive, too relentless. The way they flood every discussion, push the same talking points, drown out any criticism—it feels coordinated."

He glanced at Alice, raising an eyebrow. "Call me paranoid, but what if a lot of them are just paid bots? I wouldn't be surprised if there were companies or wealthy early adopters trying to prop up Bitcoin's narrative, making it look like this grassroots movement. But in reality? Maybe they're just protecting their investments, making sure the hype machine keeps rolling."

He sat back, arms crossed. "It's not like that kind of manipulation doesn't happen in markets all the time. And the more you think about it, the more it starts to make sense. It's easy to rally behind slogans when someone's paying you to keep shouting."

Bob nodded thoughtfully. "So, yeah, the crypto community can be pretty divided, no doubt about that. But one thing most people agree on is today's regulators, especially the SEC under *Gary Gensler*. Now, how that changes in the future, who knows? Maybe things will get better, maybe worse."

Alice tilted her head, curious. "What's the deal with the SEC, though? Why does everyone seem so worked up about them?"

Bob leaned forward, ready to explain. "The SEC—*Securities and Exchange Commission*—is the main financial regulator back home. They're responsible for enforcing laws on securities and making sure markets run smoothly. But when it comes to crypto, it's a bit of a gray area. The SEC sees a lot of cryptocurrencies as *securities*, which means they think these projects should follow strict rules like stocks or bonds. The problem is, most crypto projects didn't start out that way, and they don't want to be treated like traditional financial assets. So, the SEC is going after some of these projects, claiming they broke the rules by not registering properly."

He paused for a moment. "That's where the tension comes in. For many in crypto, the SEC's approach feels heavy-handed. People think they're stifling innovation by treating everything like it's just another stock. And when a project gets caught up in that, it can mean huge fines or even shutting down altogether."

Alice nodded slowly, processing the information. "And the maxis...?"

Bob sighed, his tone turning more cynical. "When the SEC cracks down on other cryptos, they don't just brush it off—it's more like they go out of their way to draw that line. And not just quietly either. They'll mock it, like, 'Well, serves you right for messing around with anything other than Bitcoin.' It's not just them distancing themselves; they get a kick out of throwing salt in the wound, as if to say, 'We warned you, but you didn't listen.'"

Alice laughed, catching the sharp edge in Bob's voice. "Wow, that's some real 'I told you so' energy," she said, grinning. "It's like they're not just content with being right—they've got to rub it in too, huh? But Bob, what's so bad about complying with the SEC? I mean, isn't it better to follow the rules? And how does any decision they make affect regular investors?"

Bob leaned back, considering how to frame his response. "On the surface, yeah, it seems like following the rules should be a good thing, right? But the problem is, crypto wasn't designed to fit into the traditional financial system that the SEC governs. If a project is made to comply with SEC rules, it means they would have to follow strict guidelines—register as a security, file reports, get approval for certain activities. That adds a lot of cost and slows things down."

He continued, "For big, established projects, maybe they can handle it. But for smaller, more innovative projects, that could be a death sentence. It's like trying to make them play by rules that don't really fit what they're doing. And when the SEC makes a decision to crack down on a project, it can lead to uncertainty, which impacts investor confidence."

Alice's face remained thoughtful as Bob pressed on. "And here's where general investors get hurt. If the SEC declares a token as a *security*, that token might get delisted from exchanges—especially the ones operating in the U.S.—or become unavailable for trading. Prices can plummet, and people who invested in good faith could lose a lot of money overnight. It's not just about whether a project broke a rule—it's about how the whole market reacts to the SEC's decisions."

He sighed. "So it's this tug-of-war between wanting innovation and not wanting to be crushed under regulations that might not even apply to this new technology."

Alice tilted her head, clearly puzzled. "But why would a token get delisted just because the SEC declares it a security? What's the connection?"

Bob nodded, understanding Alice's confusion. "Right, so when the SEC declares a token as a security, it doesn't just affect the exchanges that list it. The project behind the token has to start working on complying with regulations meant for securities, like filing paperwork, disclosing information, and basically proving they're not scamming investors. And that's not easy. It's expensive, time-consuming, and can quickly kill a project's momentum. Most importantly, if the SEC determines that a project is offering a security without proper registration, the team behind it could face legal consequences."

He leaned forward, emphasizing, "Additionally, many in the crypto space advocate for a decentralized financial system that prioritizes individual autonomy over government control. In fact, privacy is a huge draw for a lot of teams in the crypto space. They often prefer to operate without the scrutiny of regulators, so when they have to comply with SEC rules, they face pressure to disclose their personal and business information. This is a big deal for them because they want to maintain a certain level of anonymity and freedom in how they operate. Moreover, when a project has to comply with SEC regulations, it can feel like a betrayal of the crypto ethos."

Bob paused, adding, "And that's why some tokens get delisted. Exchanges simply don't want to deal with the risk or the hassle of having to comply with securities laws, so they just take the token down altogether."

"Now, for investors holding onto those tokens, it can be a real headache. When a token gets delisted, suddenly you can't trade it on that exchange anymore, which really limits your options for buying or selling. If the project behind that token is facing regulatory heat, it creates a lot of uncertainty about what's next. You might find it tough to cash out, and if you can only sell through sketchy platforms or peer-to-peer deals, good luck getting a decent price. Plus, if the project ends up in a legal mess, the price could drop like a rock, leaving investors with assets that might become worthless. So, yeah, delisting can really stir up a whole lot of trouble for anyone holding those tokens."

Alice raised an eyebrow, pondering Bob's explanation. "If the teams behind these projects are so focused on anonymity, doesn't that suggest they might be *hiding* something? Is that a good enough reason to think they could be fraudsters?"

Bob considered her question seriously. "That's a fair concern. I've seen many projects where the team hides behind a veil of secrecy, using anonymity as a shield for less-than-honest intentions. That's definitely something to watch out for. But, interestingly, I've also come across projects that are as transparent as they can be, and they still turn out to be complete flops. It's like they were all talk, no substance. Avoiding accountability might actually be a big reason why they want to stay anonymous. If a project fails or faces backlash, it's way too convenient for them to distance themselves from the fallout when their identities are hidden. The other reason some teams prefer anonymity is to avoid the harassment and pressure that come with being in the public eye. When people know who's behind a project, it can lead to unwanted attention, personal judgment, criticism, or even threats—especially if the project challenges the status quo."

Alice tilted her head. "So, what's the real game plan behind the SEC's moves? Are they truly champions for the investors, or is there a hidden agenda lurking beneath the surface?"

Bob leaned back, crossing his arms with a thoughtful expression. "Honestly, Alice, I don't have a clear answer. It might be both, sure—maybe they do want to protect investors. But then again, a lot of these government policies, on the surface, look like they're for our own good. Yet, when you dig deeper, you start to feel like it's more manipulative than protective. They tighten their grip, and before you know it, they're controlling the game in ways that make it harder for anyone else to play. It's like they're saying, 'We're doing this for your safety,' but there's something else going on behind the scenes."

"I mean, I don't mind if there's a win-win situation, where both sides can get what they want. But the thing is, that kind of outcome only seems possible with a fight and what really bothers me right now is that the fight feels rigged. Makes me uneasy, to be honest, like we're all pawns in a bigger chess match where they keep rewriting the rules as they go. You probably want to go read up on this alternative perspective called *Operation Choke Point 2.0*"[15]

Alice raised an eyebrow. "What's this *Operation Choke Point 2.0* you mentioned? Sounds like something out of a spy movie. What's the deal with it?"

Bob leaned forward, resting his elbows on the table. "Yeah, it's kind of dramatic, but it's not fiction. Remember the crypto guy Nic Carter? He coined the term, if I'm not mistaken. Operation Chokepoint 2.0 is basically his way of saying that the US government is trying to choke off access to the banking system for crypto companies. It's like they're not outright banning crypto, but making it so hard to operate that many projects just can't survive. The first

---

[15] https://www.piratewires.com/p/crypto-choke-point

'Operation Chokepoint' was something similar back in the early 2010s, targeting industries they didn't like by pressuring banks not to do business with them. Nic's saying the same thing is happening again, but this time with crypto. He's convinced that regulators are using this tactic to quietly suffocate the whole industry. It's a way to control or even kill it without having to pass any new laws. And personally, I don't think he would throw out any half-baked theories."

Practicality

Alice tilted her head, intrigued. "Bob, you mentioned some terms I'm not familiar with—like *decentralized applications*, *smart contracts*, and *DeFi*. What exactly do those mean?"

Bob nodded, eager to clarify. "When I talk about decentralized applications, or *dApps*, think of them like the apps you find in the *Google Play Store* or the *App Store*. There are dApps designed for trading cryptocurrencies, where you can swap tokens directly with other users without needing a centralized exchange. There are also dApps for lending and borrowing, allowing you to earn interest on your crypto or take out loans without going through a bank."

Bob noticed Alice's confusion and decided to clear things up. "Alright, let me break it down for you. Think about an app like *Spotify*. When you use it, everything you do—like the songs you play or the playlists you create—is handled by Spotify's own system. They keep track of your activity, and sure, it's private until you decide to share it. If you forget your password, you can reset it easily, and if something goes wrong, their support team can help. But, for someone who's really concerned about privacy, the fact that Spotify knows who you are and has access to your data might feel invasive. It's essentially a centralized system, meaning they control everything."

"These days, dApps have come a long way. Back in the early days, you would only access them through websites, like visiting a regular webpage. But now, you'll actually find some dApps in the App Store or Google Play Store, which makes them feel more like the apps we're used to."

"Even with that shift, dApps still work differently from something like Spotify. When you download and install Spotify, the company behind it controls everything—your data, how the app runs, all of it. With dApps, even if you download them from the app store, they run on blockchain technology behind the scenes. Instead of a company handling all the transactions and data, a decentralized network does it."

"Keep in mind, there's still a team behind the dApp. They maintain the interface you use, update features, and provide improvements, even though they don't control the actual transactions or hold your personal data. So, in that sense, you can of course argue that it's *somewhat centralized*, but the main difference is that no one can control or block your access to the dApp itself once it's on the blockchain. You're more in control than with a normal app. But if you run into trouble, there's no customer service hotline to call—Most of the support comes from the community, and you're left to figure things out on your own. So, while dApps give you more independence and privacy, they also come with that added risk."

Alice raised an eyebrow, intrigued. "That sounds interesting, but what do I need to be able to use the dApp?

Bob smiled, eager to share more. "You need a *supported* crypto wallet. Just connect your crypto wallet, and bam—you're in. It's like plug and play. No complicated registration forms or waiting for confirmation emails."

Alice looked intrigued. "That sounds simple enough, but how does it all work behind the scenes? I mean, I get that the team basically 'outsources' the data processing and recording to some decentralized blockchain networks, but what makes it possible to connect my wallet like that?"

Bob seized the opportunity to explain. "Alright, so this is where *smart contracts* come in. Picture them as digital agreements that are written into code, and they do their thing automatically when certain conditions are met. Maybe it's easier to think of a smart contract as just a bunch of mini, mini programs or bots. They're like tiny, self-operating codes that do specific tasks when certain things happen. So, when you use a dApp and connect your wallet, these little programs are working in the background, making sure everything goes smoothly. Say you're using a crypto exchange dApp to swap one coin for another. Once you send your crypto, the smart contract kicks in and sends you the equivalent amount of the other coin, no middleman needed in that process —unless you consider the smart contract itself a kind of middleman. It's all happening on the blockchain, which makes it secure and transparent."

Alice wondered aloud, "Is that kind of like an escrow service?"

Bob nodded. "Yeah, it's kind of like a 'next generation' escrow service. But instead of relying on a person or company to hold your money and make sure both sides stick to the deal, you've got code doing it. The smart contract is programmed to make sure that once you do your part, the other side has to follow through. No one can mess with it, and there's no need to trust a third party—it's all transparent and locked into the code. So yeah, it's escrow, but without the traditional middleman and with a lot more automation."

Alice, recalling their earlier discussion, asked, "Wait a second, Bob. Remember when we were talking about Bitcoin being irreversible? That could be good for sellers, but buyers might need an escrow service for protection. Now, with these smart contracts, it sounds like buyers wouldn't need to worry at all—because the smart contract works like an escrow, right?"

Bob shook his head. "Okay, I see where you're coming from, but it's a bit more nuanced. Bitcoin can handle some basic smart contract-like functions, but it's not the same as what you would find on Ethereum or other platforms. Bitcoin's smart contracts are pretty basic. It can do things like making sure everyone agrees before a transaction goes through, or allowing the coins to be spent only after a certain date. But these are pretty simple tasks. So no, Bitcoin doesn't really use smart contracts the way you're thinking."

Alice looked puzzled. "So why don't people just use smart contracts with Bitcoin?"

Bob replied, "Well, based on my understanding, Bitcoin originally prioritizes more on the *basics of money and transactions*,[16]

---

[16] Satoshi's email to Wei Dai. Subject: Re: Citation of your b-money page. Sent January 10, 2009.

rather than running programs like smart contracts. Smart contracts came later with platforms like Ethereum, which were built to handle more complex automated transactions. But now that I think about it, if there's any chance we could enable Bitcoin to handle smart contracts like Ethereum does, then why not explore that? So the question becomes: can Bitcoin actually do it? My point is that the real showstopper seems to be Bitcoin's programming language. It simply isn't capable of performing the more complex functions that smart contracts require."

He continued, "That being said, I'm sure some really smart people will come up with workarounds to get Bitcoin to handle smart contracts better. But honestly, I think Bitcoin is already so unique that it might not even need that. It has its own purpose that's different from what platforms like Ethereum offer, and maybe that's what makes it special."

Alice nodded in agreement, but then a new question popped into her mind. "But what if the smart contract code is flawed? I mean, if there's no middleman, who's responsible if something goes wrong? What happens then?"

Bob nodded, expecting the question. "That's a good point. If the code has a bug or is poorly written, there's no one to step in and fix it right away. That's one of the risks with smart contracts. Once it's out there and running on the blockchain, it's basically set in stone. If something goes wrong, you're at the mercy of that code. In traditional systems, you would call customer service, but with a smart contract, there's no one to call. That's why auditing and testing the code beforehand is crucial—because once it's live, *it's live*.".

Alice raised an eyebrow, a mix of curiosity and apprehension on her face. "So, does that mean I need to learn how to write code to understand all this?"

"Not really," Bob said. "Sure, knowing how to code helps a lot, especially if you're trying to create your own smart contracts or dApps, but you don't have to be a coding wizard to get the basics."

Alice sighed in relief, a smile spreading across her face. "Oh, that's a huge relief! I was starting to worry I would have to dive headfirst into coding just to keep up with all this. It's nice to know I can still understand the concepts without becoming a programming expert. So, what about this DeFi thingy? What exactly is that?"

Bob perked up, happy to dive in. "DeFi stands for *decentralized finance*, but I just think of it as *crypto finance*. It's like the flip side of the traditional finance world. You know how in the regular system you might borrow from banks, earn interest on savings, or invest in stocks, right? Well, with crypto finance, you're doing all that, but using *cryptocurrency* instead of regular money. The crypto industry is constantly churning out new, innovative financial products, many of which were unheard of before. And here's the thing—they're not just for 'accredited' or 'sophisticated' investors or big institutions. Anyone can access them. Most of the time, there's no need to register or fill out forms; you just need a compatible crypto wallet. These products and services run on smart contracts, so deals happen instantly."

"Now, when I say things happen instantly, I mean the transactions or deals are processed automatically by smart contracts, without the usual delays. In traditional finance, you might wait *days* for a loan approval or to transfer funds, especially if it involves paperwork, signatures, or business hours. But with DeFi, smart contracts execute agreements the moment certain conditions are met. You can get a loan, swap assets, or earn interest almost immediately, without having to wait for someone to review or sign off on anything. There's no need for any third party to approve the transaction, no waiting for a bank to open, no delays because it's a weekend. As long as the blockchain is running, these deals can happen 24/7, and once they're triggered, the transaction is done—no waiting around for someone to push a button."

"And of course no middleman, right? Because it says 'decentralized' in its name?" Alice asked.

Bob smiled. "You know, a lot of the 'no middleman' talk in DeFi comes from folks who are really excited about the idea but might not have dived into the details yet. It's easy to get caught up in the hype, but once you look closer, there's a bit more to it. When we talk about *decentralization* in DeFi, it's not just about removing banks from the picture. It might seem that way on the surface, but simply cutting out banks doesn't fully explain what decentralization means here. It's really about handing over the job to a network of independent computers that ensure 'crypto transactions' are accurately recorded in the 'crypto ledger'—the blockchain. Instead of one central entity, like a bank, processing everything, this whole global network of computers takes care of it. To me, that really gets to the heart of decentralization. And, of course, there are other aspects to consider, like the *open-source* nature of many DeFi projects, which allows anyone to inspect and contribute to the code, as well as community-driven decision-making where users have a say in the direction and *governance* of the platform."

Bob paused for a moment, then said, "I know this might sound obvious, but I'm pretty sure a lot of folks hyping up DeFi haven't really thought it through. See, even though everything runs on smart contracts, you're still relying on someone to provide the service or platform. It's not like these systems just pop out of nowhere. There's always a team behind it, making sure it all works. So in a way, there's still a 'middleman,' just in a different form. Even if people are aware of it, I think many haven't really considered how it affects them. That dependency can impact how secure or reliable things are, and it's something people tend to overlook when they get caught up in the whole 'decentralized' narrative."

"I could be wrong but I would even argue that DeFi kind of brings the 'trusted third party' back into the picture. The difference is, in most cases, you don't need to trust them to actually handle your crypto because that's where the blockchain and smart contracts take over. DeFi gets to claim that 'decentralized' label mainly because it taps into that nature of the blockchain—a decentralized and trustless system. What that really means is that blockchain allows DeFi to operate without needing a central authority to oversee transactions."

"Now, I don't want to get too caught up in the specific meaning of decentralization or dive into a debate about what truly qualifies DeFi as 'decentralized.' There's a lot of nuance to the term, and people can interpret it differently depending on how deep they go into the concept. But Alice, I think it's important to understand that, like it or not, there are still trusted third parties or individuals involved. If you don't feel comfortable with the team behind a DeFi project, it's probably a good idea to steer clear of it."

Alice nodded slowly, absorbing the information. "How about *DEX* and *CEX*?"

Bob leaned back slightly, thinking how to break it down. "Good question. So, DEX stands for *decentralized exchange*, and CEX is a *centralized exchange*. Both let you *buy* and *sell* cryptocurrencies, like a *marketplace* for crypto. But they work a bit differently."

He continued. "CEXs are designed with ease of use and customer support in mind. When you use a CEX, you create an account and then store your crypto in a digital wallet they control. That means they're holding onto your crypto for you, which comes with certain advantages. For example, when new updates happen in the crypto world, like a network upgrade or a new version of a cryptocurrency, CEXs handle all that for you. You don't have to worry about manually updating your wallet or figuring out how to deal with 'forks' in the blockchain. They take care of it behind the scenes, so your funds stay safe and everything runs smoothly."

Bob continued, "But that convenience comes with a significant risk—*custody*. When you store your crypto on a centralized exchange (CEX), you're essentially handing over control of your assets to them. If anything goes wrong, like a security breach or even a mismanagement of funds, you're at their mercy. You don't have the same level of control you would have with a personal wallet, where you're the only one holding the keys."

"Plus, there's always the chance that the exchange could face regulatory issues or even go out of business. In those cases, you might find yourself unable to access your funds. So while CEXs offer a user-friendly experience, it's important to weigh that against the potential risks of giving up custody of your crypto."

Bob smiled as he leaned back in his chair, excited to explain more. "You know, a CEX, is actually a pretty innovative product that came about thanks to the rise of crypto. It's interesting because it combines the roles of a crypto exchange and a trading platform all in one."

Alice raised an eyebrow, intrigued. "How is that innovative, though?"

Bob leaned in, clearly excited to break it down. "Alright, so in the traditional stock world, you've got two key players: the *stock exchange*, like Nasdaq or NYSE, and then the *brokerages*—like Robinhood, E*TRADE, or eToro. Now, you can't just hop onto Nasdaq and start buying stocks directly. You've got to go through a brokerage, which handles the trades for you. That means more steps, and of course, you're paying for that service."

He paused, giving Alice a moment to absorb it. "Now, with a centralized exchange, or CEX, it's different. The CEX is not only the platform where digital assets like cryptocurrencies are listed, but it also lets regular people like you and me trade directly, without needing a brokerage to do it for us. It's like if you could log into Nasdaq directly, see all the stocks, and trade them yourself—no waiting for a broker to place the order for you, no extra fees cutting into your returns. You would have full control over your trades in real time."

Bob continued, his enthusiasm growing. "Plus, the process is usually faster, which is a huge advantage when the market is moving quickly. It's a big step forward in making finance more accessible to everyone. Now, everyday people like you and me can easily join the crypto market without all the complicated stuff."

Bob continued, "Another big advantage of centralized exchanges is how they handle liquidity. You see, liquidity is basically how easily you can buy or sell an asset without causing a big impact on its price. In other words, if you want to sell your Bitcoin, you want to do it quickly and at a fair price, right?"

Alice nodded, following along. "Right. So how does a CEX come into play with that?"

Bob leaned back, clearly enjoying the discussion. "CEXs manage liquidity by pooling together a large number of buy and sell orders from all their users. This creates a more vibrant marketplace. When there are lots of people trading, it means you can usually find a buyer or seller more quickly. So, if you want to sell your Bitcoin, there's a good chance someone else on the exchange wants to buy it, making the whole process much smoother."

He paused for a moment to let that sink in. "Plus, many CEXs also have features like *market makers*—these are entities or algorithms that help ensure there are always enough orders in the market to facilitate trades. They step in to buy or sell when there's a gap, which helps maintain that liquidity and keeps the market stable."

Alice's eyes widened a bit. "Oh, I get it! So, they make sure there's always enough action happening, so trades can happen quickly and efficiently."

"Exactly." Bob was happy to see her understanding. "Without that kind of liquidity, you could end up in a situation where you want to sell but can't find anyone to buy, or you might have to lower your price significantly just to make a sale. CEXs really help mitigate those risks, making trading a lot more user-friendly."

Alice tilted her head, thinking it over. "So, *Binance* and *Coinbase*—those are CEXs, right?"

Bob nodded. "That's right. With centralized exchanges like Binance or Coinbase, they handle a lot—keeping your crypto safe, processing transactions, and even managing withdrawals. But to do all that securely, they need some of your personal info to verify who you are. That way, if you need to reset your password or take your funds out, they can confirm it's really you. It's basically like how banks work, just to make sure nobody else can access your stuff and to keep things legit on their end too."

Bob shifted the conversation slightly. "But, you know, while CEXs have their advantages, they're not without their issues. Just look at the collapse of *FTX*. It was a major centralized exchange that many people trusted. When it went down, it sent shockwaves through the entire crypto market."

Alice frowned, curious. "Yeah, I remember hearing about that. What happened exactly?"

Bob sighed, shaking his head. "Well, FTX was supposed to be a reputable player in the space. They had flashy marketing, big partnerships, and even celebrity endorsements. But behind the scenes, things were pretty messy. They were mismanaging funds, and when it came to light, it led to a massive loss of trust."

He leaned in, emphasizing his point. "That's the downside of CEXs. They handle a lot of user funds, and if their practices aren't transparent, or if they engage in risky behavior, it can lead to disaster. When FTX collapsed, it wasn't just the company that suffered; it impacted countless users who lost their money overnight."

Alice looked concerned. "So, what does that mean for other centralized exchanges?"

Bob nodded thoughtfully. "It definitely raised a lot of eyebrows. People are now even more cautious about where they're storing their crypto. It's a reminder that while CEXs offer convenience and liquidity, you need to do your homework and understand the risks. After FTX, many are looking for more transparency and security from these platforms."

Bob continued, "This brings us to the concept of *reserves*. Centralized exchanges, like FTX, are supposed to hold enough reserves to cover the assets they claim to have for their users. Think of it like a bank—there needs to be enough money in the vault for customer withdrawals. If too many people try to pull out their funds at once, like a crypto version of a bank run, and the exchange doesn't have enough reserves, it's a disaster waiting to happen. That's basically what went down with FTX. They didn't have enough on hand, and when users realized that, all trust collapsed fast."

Alice leaned back, frowning slightly. "I don't know... I mean, I love the idea of convenience and having customer support if something goes wrong, but I'm not sure if I really want to trust a centralized exchange with my crypto. What if they don't actually have the funds they say they do, like FTX?"

Bob nodded, understanding her hesitation. "Yeah, I get it. If that's your worry, you might want to consider using a DEX—a decentralized exchange. With a DEX, there's no middleman holding your crypto. You trade directly with others, so it's a more trustless system."

He continued, "Here's how it works: You connect your wallet to the DEX platform, and then you can trade directly from there. No middleman means you retain control of your funds the entire time. Plus, DEXs often have a wider variety of tokens available compared to CEXs, which can be pretty appealing."

Bob leaned in, excited to explain. "Okay, so let's break down how decentralized exchanges work a bit more, particularly the *Automated Market Maker*, or AMM, which is a key feature of many DEXs."

He paused for a moment, making sure Alice was following. "Think of an AMM like a digital pool of liquidity. Instead of matching buyers and sellers like a traditional exchange does, an AMM uses *smart contracts* to automatically set prices based on the amount of each asset in the pool."

"Here's the cool part: anyone can add their crypto to this pool, and in return, they earn a small fee from the trades that happen using their assets. It's like contributing to a community pot and getting a little something back every time someone dips into it."

Alice raised an eyebrow, interested but still a bit confused. "So, how does it decide the price?"

Bob smiled, happy to clarify. "The price is determined by a *formula* that takes into account how much of each asset is in the pool. If more people want to buy a certain token, the price goes up. If there are more sellers, the price goes down. So it's all about *supply* and *demand*, just like in any market."

He continued, "This model makes trading super-efficient, but it does have its downsides too. For example, if the market moves too quickly, you might end up with something called *slippage*, where you don't get the price you expected."

Alice furrowed her brow, still wrapping her head around it. "I don't quite get the whole idea, but as long as I can keep custody of my own crypto, I'm happy."

Bob held up a hand, a serious expression crossing his face. "Hold on, Alice. That's exactly what a lot of people think, and it can be really dangerous. Just because you're 'self-custodying' doesn't mean you're safe from risks."

Alice looked intrigued but slightly worried. "What do you mean?"

Bob leaned in, ready to explain. "First off, when you're using a DEX, you're essentially trading directly from your own crypto wallet. That means you're in control of your funds at all times, which is a great advantage. But it also means that your *seed phrase* becomes your lifeline."

Alice raised an eyebrow, intrigued. "Seed phrase? What's that?"

Bob continued. "Well, your seed phrase is like the master key to your wallet. It's a series of words—typically 12 to 24—that allows you to access your crypto. If you lose that phrase, you can't recover your wallet. If you lose your seed phrase—the secret code that gives you access to your wallet—you're basically locked out of your crypto forever. There's no customer support or help desk to call. It's gone. Imagine having a vault full of treasure and losing the key; that's how final it can be."

"So, if I decide to use a DEX, I need to make sure I have my seed phrase written down somewhere safe?" Alice asked, trying to connect the dots.

Bob replied enthusiastically. "It's not just about having it written down; you need to protect it like it's the most valuable thing you own. If someone gets hold of your seed phrase—through phishing scams or by guessing—you could lose everything. They could empty your wallet in seconds, and there's no way to reverse that."

"Yikes," Alice said, her eyes widening. "That's pretty scary."

"Exactly," Bob continued. "Then there's *phishing*. Scammers are really clever these days; they create fake websites or send emails that look just like the real deal to trick you into giving up your *private keys*. One wrong click, and your funds could vanish in an instant. These scams can be incredibly convincing, making it easy for anyone to fall for them, especially if they're not familiar with the warning signs."

Alice leaned in, curious about the terms Bob was using. "Sorry Bob but I am so confused. What's a *private key* then? Is that different from the *seed phrase*?"

Bob smiled, thinking of a simple way to explain it. "Okay, think of it this way: your wallet is like a house where you store your cryptocurrencies. Inside this house, you have different rooms. Your private key is like the key to a specific room in your house, and each room is filled with different cryptocurrencies. You need the right key to access each room and see what's inside. Now, the seed phrase is like a master key that can open all the rooms at once. It gives you access to every single cryptocurrency you have, no matter where it's stored."

"Anyway, most of us will be dealing with the seed phrase because it's what you'll use to back up and restore your wallet. Just remember to keep that spare key safe, as losing it means you could be locked out of your own home—your crypto, in this case"

"Wow, that sounds like a lot of responsibility," Alice remarked. "It's almost like I'm my own bank."

"That's one way to look at it," Bob chuckled. "But with that responsibility comes the need for vigilance. Just remember: with great power comes great responsibility."

Alice nodded slowly, her expression thoughtful. "I see what you mean. What else?"

"Let's not forget about the plethora of scam coins out there," Bob said. "Some projects might look shiny and promising at first glance, but they're often just traps designed to steal your money. It's kind of like diving into a startup without doing any background checks—you could easily find yourself investing in something that's nothing more than an outright fraud or a *Ponzi* scheme. If you decide to put your crypto into one of those scam coins, there's a good chance you might never see that money again."

Alice chuckled at the mention of a 'Ponzi scheme.'

"Funny you say that, because a lot of people claim crypto itself is a Ponzi scheme. It's like a Ponzi scheme *within* a Ponzi scheme!"

Bob chuckled when he heard Alice's comment about Ponzi schemes. "You know," he said, grinning, "when people call crypto a Ponzi scheme, I actually find it amusing. It's interesting how some people can be so unaware." He leaned back, preparing to explain further.

Bob leaned forward, eyes glinting with intensity. "You know, there's a scheme out there that's even worse than a Ponzi scheme. It's so well-disguised, so deeply embedded in how the world operates, that people don't even question it."

Alice raised an eyebrow, intrigued. "What are you talking about?"

Bob continued. "You become a member of the *scheme* by handing over your hard-earned money, because hey, that's just what everyone does, right? Now, you've got your eye on your dream house, so you go to the scheme for help. They're all smiles and say, 'Sure, we can help you out! But, you know, we've got our CEOs, executives, staff, and investors to pay, not to mention keeping our fancy offices running, so we can't do it for free.' Then they offer you a deal: 'How about you tell us which house you want, we'll buy it from the seller, sell it back to you at a higher price, and call it even?' But here's the deal: 'We know you don't have that kind of money lying around, so don't worry—you can pay us back in monthly installments. Meanwhile, go ahead and move in, but remember—we're technically the landlord until you're fully paid up. And if you miss those payments? Well, we'll have to ask you to pack up and leave.' You think it over and say, 'Fair enough,' and just like that, you've signed up."

"What's really wild is that the members of the scheme are the ones doing all the legwork. They go out, find valuable properties or assets on their own, then bring them to the scheme. The scheme steps in as a middleman, buys those properties, and then turns around to sell them back to the same members—at a marked-up price, of course. So, essentially, the members are sourcing their own deals and then paying the scheme extra for the privilege of getting what they found in the first place. It's almost like a cult offering from the members. The more they offer to the scheme, the more they are 'in debt' to the scheme."

"But here's the real kicker: this entire scheme has the government's blessing to create money out of absolutely nothing—no gold, no assets, not even physical cash backing it. It's just numbers in a system. So, when people buy and sell, the scheme isn't moving real money around; it's just updating numbers in accounts. It's like playing a game where the currency isn't even real, but everyone agrees to treat it like it is. And the craziest part? If the scheme ever collapses under its own weight—whether it's due to poor management or risky investments—they don't have to worry. They've got government support, ready to swoop in and bail them out with taxpayer money. It's like having a guaranteed safety net, so no matter how reckless or irresponsible they are with your money, they'll never face the full consequences."

Alice laughed, catching on. "Wait, I think I get what you're saying. You're saying the traditional banking system is kind of like a Ponzi scheme? That's a crazy idea, don't you think?" she asked, her eyes wide with surprise.

Bob nodded, smiling. "Well, it operates in ways that would make most actual Ponzi schemes blush, but it's so normalized that no one bats an eye."

He continued, leaning back with a smirk. "The whole system runs on debt, and most people don't realize that their money is constantly being lent out and multiplied, but not necessarily in their favor. In fact, the entire economy is built on the assumption that people will keep borrowing and paying back their loans. But if that chain breaks—if too many people default, or if people lose confidence in the system—it could all come crashing down. And who's left holding the bag? Ordinary people, like you and me."

Alice sat back, processing what Bob had just said. "That… actually *does* sound a lot like a Ponzi scheme," she murmured. "Everyone keeps putting money in, hoping it all holds together, but it's really just balancing on a knife's edge. So, when people call crypto a Ponzi scheme…"

Bob shrugged. "They're either turning a blind eye or don't realize that the system they're defending operates in almost the same way. Maybe they're fine with it because, in some way, they're the ones benefiting from it."

Alice leaned in, raising an eyebrow. "So… with crypto, you've got more control and can actually see what's going on—of course only if you know your way around it. But with traditional finance, you're just kind of stuck trusting a system that keeps most of its gears hidden behind a lot of fancy talk and paperwork. Right?" She glanced at Bob, looking for a sign she was on the right track.

Bob nodded, a small smile forming. "Exactly. You've got it."

Alice stared at him, the wheels clearly turning in her head. "Wait a minute, Bob. Are you kind of dodging my question here? Even if traditional banking is as bad as a Ponzi scheme, that doesn't exactly clear crypto's name—what makes it any different?"

Bob chuckled. "Good point, Alice. Just because one system has flaws doesn't automatically make the other perfect. But here's why crypto stands apart."

He leaned in, his tone more earnest now. "In a Ponzi scheme, the people at the top pocket returns by using the money from new participants to pay earlier investors. When fresh money stops coming in, the whole thing falls apart because no actual value is being created—just a closed loop of money changing hands."

Alice nodded, following him. "Right, that's the basic setup."

Bob looked her in the eye. "So, who do you think benefits from the rise of crypto? Is it just some centralized group pulling the strings?"

Alice thought for a moment. "Based on what you've told me, no, it's mostly the community that benefits—assuming it's not some scam project."

Bob smiled. "So does that address your question?"

Alice crossed her arms, still skeptical. "Not entirely. I can't help thinking about all the people throwing money into Bitcoin and other cryptos, waiting for a big payday. It feels like they're chasing after something that could collapse at any time. And when I hear talk about the 'hyped' and 'speculative' value of crypto, it does make me wonder if it's a Ponzi scheme in disguise." She looked at him, thoughtful. "It's hard to shake that feeling when you see people banking on the market just taking off."

Bob leaned back, nodding slowly as he considered Alice's point. "You're right to be skeptical, and it's interesting you brought that up. If you think about it, the stock market isn't all that different."

"Think about it: in the stock market, when a company launches an innovative product or makes bold promises about future growth, investors can get swept up in the excitement, just like with crypto.

The media buzz, social media trends, and even endorsements from influential figures can create this illusion of value that isn't really grounded in reality. It's like everyone's chasing after the next big thing, not really realizing that the whole system can be a bit shaky. The stock price can soar based on that excitement, even before the company actually earns a dime from those future prospects."

"So, you have this scenario where billions can be added to a company's market capitalization overnight, just because people think it's going to be the next big thing. And that inflated value can feel very real to those who are riding the wave. But what are we really talking about? If you want to be critical, it's 'fake' or 'phantom' wealth created from expectations rather than actual cash flow."

"Now, when you look at the crypto market, it operates on a similar principle. The excitement around new projects, the promise of decentralized finance, and the hope of future use cases can drive prices sky-high, too. But because it's a newer space, people are quicker to label it as a Ponzi scheme when it behaves the same way the stock market does."

"It's almost ironic. Both systems create wealth based on trust and belief, yet the traditional stock market is seen as a legitimate means of investing, while crypto gets a bad rap. So, it begs the question—why do we accept one but not the other? It feels like a real contradiction in how society views different types of investment."

Alice tilted her head, narrowing her eyes. "Bob, it sounds like you're talking about penny stocks, you know? Those risky companies that are all hype and no substance. But that's not the same as *blue-chip* stocks—the big names. Those have real value. They're backed by assets, revenue, and decades of growth. People aren't just speculating there; they're investing in something tangible."

Bob nodded, acknowledging her point. "You're right. Blue-chip stocks are grounded in real assets and stable revenue. They have an established value that's backed by actual operations, cash flow, and often even dividends. But even blue-chip companies can have inflated stock prices, sometimes based more on sentiment than on performance. Look at tech giants; their valuations can surge because of future potential rather than just current earnings."

Alice crossed her arms, a thoughtful look on her face. "But here's the thing, Bob. At least in the traditional stock market, those companies are backed by tangible assets or products. There's something concrete behind those shares, right? What about crypto? What's backing that value?"

Bob nodded, acknowledging her point. "I get what you're saying, Alice. It makes sense to want something solid to lean on when you're investing. But let's dig a bit deeper. Many companies in the stock market, especially tech startups, don't always have physical assets either. They often start off with little more than a concept and a team. Investors pour money in based on belief in that idea, and if the company takes off, the value skyrockets, regardless of any physical assets."

"Sure, crypto doesn't have the usual backing we're familiar with, but it's all about shaking things up and doing something revolutionary, thanks to the strong support of its community. It resonates with people on multiple levels, offering a solution that directly addresses their unmet needs. Who are we to say this isn't a tangible product in action?"

Alice raised an eyebrow, clearly not convinced. "You know, if it were up to me, I would rather pick gold or silver over crypto any day. At least those precious metals have intrinsic value. They're real, tangible assets that people have trusted for centuries."

Bob nodded thoughtfully. "I understand why you would choose gold or silver—they've been valued for a long time. But isn't it a bit outdated to cling to those shiny rocks? Sure, they have intrinsic value, but many people don't realize that it's mostly about how we can use them as raw materials for consumer products. Are we really saying crypto isn't raw material for a new wave of financial products? Just like gold and silver are used in electronics, jewelry, and even medicine, crypto can underpin an entire ecosystem of decentralized applications, smart contracts, and digital assets. So, when we talk about intrinsic value, maybe we should consider how crypto is becoming a vital part of the tech landscape. It's not just digits on a screen; it's the backbone of a financial revolution that's creating new possibilities and efficiencies in ways we're only beginning to understand. So, who's to say crypto isn't the new gold?"

Then, Bob leaned back, a thoughtful expression crossing his face. "You know, Alice, here's another interesting perspective: in many countries, including ours, crypto trading is considered legitimate and regulated. So when someone calls crypto a Ponzi scheme, are they essentially accusing the very authorities that permit stock trading of endorsing a Ponzi scheme too? That's a pretty bold statement, don't you think?"

Alice raised an eyebrow, intrigued by his point. "That's a compelling argument. It really makes you question the consistency of that label."

"Exactly," Bob continued, warming to the topic. "It's a self-contradictory claim. Just because crypto can be volatile or speculative doesn't mean it's fraudulent. The authorities that regulate these markets are recognizing their potential. If they believe that crypto can coexist with traditional investments, what does that say about those who are quick to dismiss it as a scam?"

Alice nodded, her curiosity piqued. "I see your point. If a government legitimizes crypto trading, it suggests they believe there's real value and integrity in it."

"Precisely," Bob replied, leaning in slightly. "When people throw around the term 'Ponzi scheme,' it often reflects their biases or misunderstandings rather than a well-informed critique. It's a convenient label to dismiss something they don't fully understand. But if they're going to use that term, they should consider what it implies about their own traditional investments and the systems they're part of. Are they questioning the legitimacy of the stock market and the institutions overseeing it?"

Alice smiled thoughtfully. "That definitely adds another layer to the discussion. It's easy to write something off as a scam without digging deeper. I guess just because there are scams in crypto doesn't mean the entire system is a scam, just like traditional finance has its own set of issues too."

Bob smiled, happy to see her understanding deepen. "Right! It all comes down to being informed and careful with where you put your money, whether in crypto or traditional finance."

Just as Alice was about to ask her next question, the barista came over to their table with a small plate of pastries and spoke in rapid Japanese, nodding at Bob and gesturing to the treats. Bob smiled back, nodding in thanks. He then turned to Alice. "She's offering us these for free—apparently, they had extras today."

Alice's eyes lit up. "Oh, that's awesome! Thank you so much!" She beamed at the barista, who gave a polite nod before heading back behind the counter.

As Alice picked up a pastry, savoring the unexpected treat, she looked over at Bob with a grin. "You know, little surprises like this are kind of magical."

"True," Bob replied. "But in trading, surprises aren't always this sweet."

She raised an eyebrow, intrigued. "Oh?"

He explained. "There's this thing called *slippage*. This occurs when the price of an asset shifts between the time you place a trade and when it actually gets executed. In a volatile market, you might think you're buying Bitcoin at a solid price, but by the time your order goes through, the price could have surged. Suddenly, you end up paying significantly more—or receiving less if you're selling. It's frustrating, especially when you're trying to maximize your trades."

"So, like, if I ordered pastries during a promotional hour, expecting a discount, but by the time I went to pay, the promotion had ended, and I got charged the full price? she asked, half-joking.

"Yes, that's pretty close," he laughed, recalling a recent experience. "Let me give you a real-life example of slippage that I encountered while using a decentralized exchange. A few weeks ago, I was trying to buy some Bitcoin just after a significant market dip. I saw a price I liked on the DEX and decided to place my order for a decent amount."

"So, I connected my wallet to the DEX dApp and set the amount I wanted to buy. I even checked the price chart to confirm that I was making a good move. I hit 'swap' and confirmed the transaction, but as the order was processing, I noticed the price started to move up rapidly. It turns out that there was a surge in buying activity on the platform right after I placed my order."

"When my transaction finally executed, I ended up paying nearly 5% more than the price I initially saw. It was incredibly frustrating because I had thought I was making a smart move by acting quickly."

"Overall, slippage is just one of those factors that can catch you off guard in a fast-moving market. You think you're making a smart decision, but the reality is that the market can shift in an instant."

Alice exclaimed, "Wow, that sounds really frightening! Is there any way to avoid slippage?"

Bob continued, "To avoid slippage in the future, there are a few strategies I've picked up along the way. First, one of the simplest ways is to set a slippage tolerance when you're placing your order. Most decentralized exchanges allow you to specify how much price movement you're willing to accept before the trade goes through. For instance, if you set it to 1% and the price moves beyond that during execution, the transaction will just fail instead of going through at a worse price."

"Second, timing is key. If you're planning to make a trade, you probably want to try to do it during periods of lower volatility or when the market is less active. This can help minimize those rapid price changes that lead to slippage."

"Third, consider breaking up larger trades into smaller ones. Instead of placing a big order all at once, splitting it into smaller orders can sometimes reduce the impact of slippage. It allows you to take advantage of different price points and can prevent the market from reacting too strongly to your order."

"Finally, keep an eye on the liquidity of the trading pair you're dealing with. If you're trading a less popular asset or a pair with low liquidity, you're more likely to experience slippage. In those cases, it might be better to wait for a better time or choose a more liquid asset."

Alice bit her lip, her earlier confidence wavering. "So, while self-custody sounds good in theory, there's a lot I need to consider, huh?"

"Definitely," Bob said, giving her a reassuring nod. "It's all about being prepared and vigilant. If you decide to go that route, just make sure you educate yourself on how to protect your assets."

Alice leaned in, her enthusiasm bubbling over. "Alright, I'm sold! If I want to jump into the crypto world, how do I get my hands on some? What's the first step on this wild adventure?"

Bob leaned in, a playful glint in his eye. "Alright, Alice, have you ever played *Minecraft*?"

Alice chuckled. "Yeah, I used to build these ridiculous castles and got way too good at dodging *Creepers*. But what's Minecraft got to do with buying crypto?"

Bob smiled. "Bear with me for a second. You know the *Nether Portal*, right? That purple, swirling gateway you step into to enter the Nether?"

Alice nodded. "Of course. The portal's how you get to a whole other world."

"Exactly," Bob continued, "the Nether Portal is your way to cross between two different realms—the regular Minecraft overworld and the strange, new Nether. And when it comes to crypto, it's a lot like that. Crypto exists in its own 'realm'—one that's different from our regular money world."

Alice raised an eyebrow. "So… what's my Nether Portal in the real world?"

Bob leaned back and grinned. "That's where things like a centralized exchange, or even your credit card, come in. They're your 'Nether Portals' to the crypto world. By using them, you're basically stepping through a gateway, converting your regular dollars into crypto that you can actually use in the other 'world.' They're how you bring your traditional money over to the crypto side."

Alice considered this, a smile slowly forming. "So, if I wanted to start my crypto adventure, I would just go through a portal—like on Coinbase or with my credit card?"

"Exactly. Think of it like gathering resources before you head through the portal in Minecraft. Once you're set up, you're ready to step into the crypto world."

Seeing Alice nodding along, Bob decided to go a bit deeper. "So, here's where it gets a little technical. Those portals we talked about? In the crypto world, we call them *on-ramps* and *off-ramps*."

Alice tilted her head. "On-ramps and off-ramps? Like… actual ramps?

"Exactly!" Bob grinned. "Imagine a highway ramp connecting two different parts of a city. When you want to bring your regular money into the crypto world, you take an 'on-ramp'—usually through a centralized exchange like Coinbase or Binance, or sometimes even with a credit card. It's how you *enter* the crypto space."

Alice's face lit up in understanding. "And when I want to *exit* the crypto space? Like, cash out—"

"You would use an 'off-ramp,'" Bob finished, nodding. "If you want to convert your crypto back to regular money, that's when you would take that off-ramp, using the exchange again to get back into dollars or your regular currency."

Alice smiled, clearly enjoying the analogy. "I guess I've got my road map now. On-ramps, off-ramps… and a few Nether Portals in between."

JKAA

Future

Alice gazed out the cafe window at the quiet, orderly streets of Shibuya. "It's so beautiful here," she said, a hint of wistfulness in her voice. "Everything feels so calm and... in place. Back home, things are pretty chaotic these days. People are divided on everything—freedom has kind of spiraled out of control. And the worst part is that some people are even turning to violence to sort things out. I don't know... it just feels like we're losing something."

Bob nodded, sensing the heaviness behind her words. After a pause, Alice turned back to him. "Have you ever thought about moving, as in 'migrating' to Japan for good? I mean, you seem so at home here."

He shook his head. "I get why it seems that way, but no, I could never settle here permanently. I still love home too much, with all its messiness and challenges."

Alice gave him a warm smile. Just then, Bob's expression shifted as if something had clicked. "But, you know," he continued, "there's something interesting going on. In a way, we're in the middle of a different kind of migration—a financial one."

Alice tilted her head, intrigued. "What do you mean?"

"Well, the world is starting to shift from traditional money systems to crypto. It's like a global financial migration. People are exploring new ways to handle value, ownership, and transactions—just like the movement of people searching for something better. It's the same urge for freedom and new possibilities, but in finance."

Alice leaned forward, fascinated. "So, you're saying this isn't just about investing or speculating—it's like an actual movement?"

"Exactly. It's a migration from one system to another, fueled by people looking for something that traditional finance isn't giving them. It's still tied to old systems in some ways, but it's leading us somewhere new. And just like any migration, it'll have its own challenges and growing pains."

Bob took a moment, his gaze drifting to the busy yet orderly streets of Shibuya before continuing.

"Think about it this way," he said, leaning in a little closer. "Traditional finance is like this big, established city. It has banks, regulations, tons of infrastructure, and it's been built up over centuries. People know how to navigate it—even if they're not always happy with it."

Alice nodded, following his analogy.

He continued. "But crypto? It's more like a new frontier. It has some buildings, maybe a few paths carved out, but it's still mostly open land. And while that's exciting, it also means there aren't as many safeguards. People are flocking here because they believe in what they can build, or maybe they're frustrated with the limits of that 'old city.' But at the same time, they're bringing with them the need for things they're used to: stability, security, and speed."

Alice tilted her head thoughtfully. "So people want to bring in the best of the old world but are willing to embrace the values of this new one?"

Bob nodded. "Exactly. They're committed to adapting to the new values—decentralization, privacy, and autonomy—while still finding ways to make it feel secure."

She smiled, processing it. "It's like they're holding onto some familiar tools to feel anchored, but they're willing to learn a new way of living."

Bob leaned in, a serious note in his voice. "And that's a big part of the tension you see in the crypto world. The community—the people who have 'migrated' to this new financial territory—they're here because they believe in the potential for true freedom, autonomy, and a decentralized way of operating. So, when they see certain groups or even governments trying to bring back old ways—centralized control, regulations that feel restrictive—it feels like they're trying to turn this open, new city back into the one they left."

Alice raised her eyebrows, clearly intrigued.

"Imagine building a life in this exciting, expansive place where you're free to try new things, take charge of your assets, and not rely on big institutions," he continued. "And then suddenly, someone comes in saying, 'Actually, we should put up a few more checkpoints, add more gates, bring in a central authority to manage things.' It's almost like a betrayal of what they came here for."

Alice nodded thoughtfully. "So, it's like people want to live by the new rules but can't escape the pull of the old world wanting to rein things in."

"Exactly," Bob replied. "That's where a lot of the frustration comes from. People who embrace this migration to crypto want to build something new—while others are trying to make it conform to the old ways. And that tension? It's shaping the future of finance as we know it. And that's where it gets even more complicated. On one hand, you have people who want crypto to be completely separate—no banks, no government involvement. But then there's the practical side: to buy your first crypto, you need regular money, right? Think about it—almost everyone has dollars, yen, euros, but not everyone has Bitcoin or Ethereum just sitting around. When people buy crypto, they're often still measuring its worth in terms of dollars or their local currency. For now, that bridge between them—the on-ramps and off-ramps, like banks and exchanges—has to exist for this migration to even be possible. It's not just a clean break—it's a transition. And until crypto finds its footing as a standalone economy, it'll keep needing those connections. It's a bit like training wheels for this new financial world."

Alice raised an eyebrow and leaned forward, "So, if someone really wanted to stop this migration, couldn't they just… break the ramps?"

Bob gave a wry smile. "Funny you mention that—that's actually happening. Think about it. Banks, regulators, even entire governments are starting to put up blockades. They're making it harder to transfer regular money into crypto. They're tightening regulations, limiting credit card transactions, shutting down bank accounts linked to exchanges. It's like they're trying to dismantle the on-ramps and off-ramps, piece by piece, hoping it'll stop people from even thinking about crossing over."

Alice's eyes widened. "So, they're kind of barricading the bridge to the new world?"

"Exactly," Bob nodded. "It's a way to control the flow, to make sure this migration doesn't get too far out of their reach. For example, by making it difficult to buy or sell crypto using traditional money, they're slowing down adoption, or at least making it way more challenging. In fact, they've come up with another approach… They're migrating along, in a sense."

Alice looked intrigued. "Migrating along? How do you mean?"

"Exactly. They're planning to join it themselves by introducing their own versions of digital currency. This is where things like *Central Bank Digital Currencies*, or CBDCs, come in. Governments are working on their own form of digital money that looks and functions a bit like crypto but is backed by their central banks."

Alice raised her eyebrows, "So they're building their own little digital city inside the new world?"

"Exactly," Bob nodded. "It's like they're saying, 'If people are going to migrate, we'll build a nice spot for them to land.' But it's not the same as crypto, where the control is distributed among the users themselves. With CBDCs, the central authority is still very much in charge. They can monitor every transaction, restrict how and when you spend, and even limit what you can buy in certain cases. It's the government's way of adapting to the digital shift while holding onto control."

Alice looked thoughtful. "I guess they're trying to get a say in how it unfolds. So, people might end up in this 'new world' but still be tied to the rules of the old one? "

"Pretty much," Bob replied. "It's like migrating to a new city but finding out the government has moved right along with you, keeping the same rules in place. It's an interesting move—and one that'll be fascinating to watch."

Alice looked thoughtful, then asked, "But wait—if we're already using mobile payments and credit cards, isn't that already digital money? I mean, I rarely even use cash anymore. What's the difference with CBDCs?"

Bob nodded, seeing where she was coming from. "Good question. I get why it seems that way—when you're using a mobile app or credit card, it *feels* like digital money, but it's actually just *digital payments*," he said.

"Digital payments?" Alice prompted, intrigued.

"Right," Bob continued. "When you tap your phone or swipe your card, the process is digital, but the actual money behind it is essentially still moving through the traditional banking system. Your bank verifies you have enough funds, then sends it to the merchant's bank. Banks are the ones handling and tracking it all in their ledgers. So, the money is only *sort of* digital—it's still tied to that system."

Alice tilted her head, processing. "So, what's different with a CBDC then?"

"With a CBDC," Bob explained, "the digital money would be issued and managed directly by the central bank, just like cash. It wouldn't require any commercial bank involvement to verify or transfer. You would get it straight into a digital wallet controlled by the central bank, and it would be fully digital from the start. It's not just that the process is digital but it is a real digital money."

"So, it's like direct, government-issued digital cash?" Alice asked.

"Exactly," Bob replied, "a CBDC would act as true digital money—like cash but digital—allowing the government to control and track it all in real-time, which is a big shift from today's system. But, having said that, other than crypto, there is actually a kind of 'digital money' already 'circulating' in the market right now."

Alice raised an eyebrow. "Wait—like what?"

Bob nodded. "Well, think about how banks operate with *fractional reserve banking*. They're essentially allowed to 'create' money by lending out more than they actually have on deposit. So, in a way, they're creating digital money whenever they approve a loan or add funds to someone's account. It's 'backed' *only* by the bank—not by an asset, necessarily, but by trust that the system will hold up and the bank will honor its obligations. But unlike crypto or CBDCs, this 'digital money' is entirely within the bank's system."

He leaned in, his voice a little lower. "This so-called 'digital money' created by banks is probably the worst kind of digital money, if you think about it. It's like this... almost *fake* money, created out of thin air through loans and credits, with nothing really behind it but the bank's word. And yet, no one questions it because we're used to it—it's just how the system's always worked. With crypto, at least, what you see is what you get. There's no magic multiplication happening behind the scenes."

He continued, now with a bit of a smirk playing on his face. "Now, with CBDCs, the government is essentially doing the same thing—creating money out of thin air. Again, it's not backed by anything tangible in the market; it's just 'trust us' written in digital form. They can issue as much as they want without needing reserves, just based on what they think the economy needs."

Alice's eyes widened, and she let out a small laugh of realization. "So... it's basically a smart way for the government to print money without physically printing it."

"Bingo," Bob replied. "Only, this time, they're calling it *innovation*."

Alice raised an eyebrow. "But hold on—if the U.S. issued a CBDC, it wouldn't really be the same as the cash dollar, right? I mean, they're different forms, so wouldn't that mean it wouldn't impact the actual value of money in circulation? Like, the cash and CBDC would exist separately, so it's not like they're 'diluting' the value of each other... or are they?"

Bob shook his head, a slight smile on his face. "Not quite. A CBDC would still be just as much a dollar as the cash in your wallet because its value is directly tied to the U.S. dollar. So, if they issued a CBDC, it's like adding more dollars to the money supply—just in digital form. It might feel separate, but it's essentially expanding the total number of dollars out there, just in a new, controlled layer. It's a powerful move—and, honestly, a little unsettling when you think about what that could mean for us."

Bob leaned back, his tone more serious. "Now, when you consider that the government can print both USD and CBDCs, combined with the banks creating their own 'digital money,' it becomes clear that we're truly living in a bubble economy. And I am not going to lie, I believe Bitcoin and other cryptocurrencies are part of the picture, too. The lines between what's real and what's artificially inflated are getting blurrier by the day."

Alice raised an eyebrow, a playful smile tugging at her lips. "So, tell me—would you rather see this bubble burst and watch the whole thing 'reset,' or do you think it's better if it just keeps floating along?"

Bob leaned back, a wry grin crossing his face. "You know, part of me thinks a reset would be a wake-up call. But then, it would be absolute chaos. I honestly don't know what's better. But I'll tell you what I am sure of: I need to keep my debt low, spend wisely, save smartly, and invest cautiously. That's the only plan I have right now. People forget that managing your spending is just as important as investing or saving. If you're careful with what you spend on, you're already ahead of the game. Because in the end, a steady budget and thoughtful spending can weather more storms than we realize. We'll probably need it if this bubble really does burst one day."

Alice chuckled, leaning in with a spark of mischief. "So no big bets on Bitcoin or some startup changing the world overnight, then?"

Bob laughed. "Not a chance. I mean, a little in crypto, maybe, but definitely not an all-in kind of thing. It's like gambling; you might make a little, but I would rather not bank on it."

She tilted her head thoughtfully. "Okay, so if you're going cautious, where do you think people will find stability if the bubble pops? Like, what's worth holding on to in that kind of world?"

Bob grew thoughtful, looking down at his coffee. "Probably the basics. Food, energy, practical things people need. A garden in the backyard might be more valuable than a stock portfolio if things get really rough."

He continued, "You know, that so-called 'wealth' people talk about? It's often just *on-paper* wealth. It's all about the numbers flashing on their screens. When someone brags about how much their Bitcoin is worth, it's pretty unsettling when you think about it."

"It means that one day, someone's hard-earned money could be swallowed up by those inflated valuations. If the market shifts, that 'wealth' could vanish in an instant. It's not like it's safely stashed in a bank account; it's tied up in a volatile market that can swing dramatically with just a tweet or a news headline."

"People need to realize those valuations only hold weight as long as the market perceives them that way. If everyone decides to sell at once, that 'wealth' can disappear just as fast as it appeared. We really need a realistic view of what wealth means, especially in the unpredictable world of crypto."

Alice listened closely, the weight of Bob's words sinking in. "So, it's about being cautious and not getting swept up in the hype?"

"Exactly," Bob nodded. "Staying grounded and understanding the risks is crucial. All this talk about wealth misses the bigger picture. What does 'wealth' really mean in a world where so many people are just trying to secure basic needs like food and shelter? It's almost absurd when you think about it. Those soaring Bitcoin prices don't mean much when the foundation of society—basic necessities—is starting to crumble."

"People get so caught up in their on-paper wealth that they lose sight of what truly matters. When the economy gets rocky, those luxuries can become irrelevant if you can't secure food or shelter. Wealth should be more than just numbers; it should enable a stable and sustainable life for everyone."

Alice nodded, absorbing Bob's perspective. "So, it's about finding balance and recognizing real value beyond just money."

"Exactly," Bob said, his voice tinged with urgency. "*True wealth* should contribute to a better world, not just inflate someone's ego or status. And you know what? I genuinely believe the wealth gap between the rich and the poor is only going to widen, and unfortunately, crypto might play a big part in that."

"Think about it. While some people get rich off their investments, many are left behind, unable to join this digital gold rush. The irony is that crypto was meant to promote decentralization and equal opportunity, yet it often deepens existing inequalities. Those who can afford to invest or understand the technology get richer, while those without access or knowledge are left in the dust."

"Look, I'm not saying wealth should be equally distributed—that's unrealistic. People have different skills, ambitions, and circumstances; that's just how the world works. But we're heading toward a scenario where disparity is growing more extreme. The rich are getting richer, and the poor are getting poorer, creating a snowball effect. As the wealthy accumulate more, they can invest in more opportunities, while those who struggle are left with fewer options."

"And when people start feeling that unfairness, things can get chaotic. Frustration builds, creating a breeding ground for resentment. When the gap between the haves and the have-nots becomes too stark, people may start to feel lawless, like the system is rigged against them. That's a dangerous cycle that can lead to unrest and societal breakdown."

Alice contemplated Bob's words. "So, you're saying the very technology meant to empower people could end up hurting them?"

"Yes," Bob replied, his tone serious. "It's a double-edged sword."

Alice chuckled, raising an eyebrow. "So, should I start stockpiling some Japanese instant ramen just in case? You know, for the impending ramen apocalypse?"

Bob laughed, appreciating her humor. "Hey, you might be onto something! At least you'll be prepared while the rest of us are lost in the bubble."

She raised her coffee cup, clinking it against his. "Cheers to practical wisdom, then."

"Cheers," he replied, smiling.

The café's atmosphere—a warm, inviting space filled with the scent of freshly brewed coffee—seemed to cradle their deeper conversation, adding a sense of balance and intimacy to the moment. They sat in comfortable silence for a bit, watching the world outside pass by, each lost in their own thoughts, yet somehow connected by the weight of their discussion.

Epilogue

The golden light of the setting sun streamed through the café window, casting long shadows across the table. Alice sat back, her mind buzzing with newly gained insights, a curious mix of wonder and confusion swirling within her. Part of her didn't want the conversation to end; she felt as if they were only scratching the surface of something vast and mysterious.

"This has been... fascinating," she said, her voice sincere. "I never imagined crypto could be so complex, yet strangely captivating."

Bob smiled, a flicker of pride in his tired eyes. Seeing Alice, almost on the edge of becoming a crypto enthusiast, gave him a renewed sense of purpose. "Well, it's not every day I get to share this with someone who's genuinely curious."

Alice glanced at the clock, realizing how time had slipped away. "It's wild how fast this day flew by. I feel like I could sit here and listen to your explanations forever."

Bob chuckled softly, leaning back. "Yeah, same here. But real life calls."

She let out a playful sigh. "And now I'm left to unravel this maze on my own," she joked, though there was a genuine undertone of apprehension.

"Don't worry," Bob said, a reassuring note in his voice. "Take your time. It's not about diving in all at once. It's about discovery, in your own way."

Alice nodded, feeling comforted. "Thanks for that. You've made it a little less intimidating, at least."

EPILOGUE

As they gathered their belongings, an unexpected quiet settled between them, filled with things unspoken yet deeply felt. Bob looked out at the city streets, full of life and mystery. "So, what's next for you?" he asked.

Alice's eyes lit up. "*Kyoto*, tomorrow," she said. "I want to explore the temples, maybe catch some cherry blossoms. Everyone says it's magical this time of year."

Bob could picture her wandering through the ancient gardens, the cherry blossoms drifting like snowflakes. "You'll love it," he said, his voice soft. "Take your time. Let it all sink in."

A touch of wistfulness crossed her face. "It's funny, though. Even an adventure like this feels too short."

Bob nodded, the weight of that truth settling in. "Yeah. But that's what makes each moment matter." He paused, his gaze steady. "Just like crypto—exploration leads to discovery."

She smiled, and something unspoken passed between them, a spark of shared understanding. "I'll miss these talks," Alice said, almost to herself.

"Me too," Bob replied, a rare seriousness in his voice. "But hey, let's stay in touch. I'd love to hear where your journey takes you, both in life and... maybe even in crypto."

Alice's heart warmed. "I'd like that. This trip wouldn't have been the same without you."

They stepped into the cool, vibrant evening, the sky a deepening canvas of colors. The city thrummed with possibility. Exchanging numbers, they made loose promises to share stories of adventures yet to come. There was a sense of finality but also the unmistakable whisper of new beginnings.

"Take care, Alice," Bob said, his voice layered with sincerity.

She grinned, a spark of excitement in her eyes. "You too, Bob. Let's see where all this takes us."

EPILOGUE

They parted ways, each carrying a piece of the other in their hearts. As Alice disappeared into the Tokyo twilight, the streets seemed to glow a little brighter, alive with the promise of uncharted adventures, both in the world of cryptocurrency and whatever lay beyond.

Afterword

So, here we are at the end of the story. Along the way, I hope you picked up some fascinating insights about crypto. Before we wrap up, I wanted to share a bit of what I personally think about crypto. With all the buzz, I still think it's a pretty risky investment, especially with all the uncertainty around where regulators stand. Sure, risk comes with opportunity, but I would never put my entire savings into it. I make sure to have at least 24 months' worth of emergency savings set aside. Maybe that sounds a bit extreme, but the *Covid* pandemic taught me to be prepared for anything. And honestly, 24 months isn't that much if you're willing to cut back on spending when times get tough.

In the crypto world, much like traditional finance, there are endless promises of quick riches and groundbreaking strategies. Flashy headlines and online influencers tout sky-high returns, and get-rich-quick schemes abound, preying on people's hopes and vulnerabilities—just like those old carnival scams.

With that in mind, I would like to share something the late *Charlie Munger* once said,[17] which is worth reflecting on, even for crypto enthusiasts. And yes, I'm aware Munger wasn't a fan of crypto; he even called it 'crap' on TV. And he's not alone—*Warren Buffett* famously labeled Bitcoin as 'an asset that creates nothing.' It's a bit sad that such prominent investors don't see crypto the way many of us do. But given their decades of extraordinary success in stock investing, who are we to say they don't have some valuable lessons for us? Let's see if there's a nugget of wisdom we can apply to our own crypto journeys.

---

[17] YouTube @FREEINVESTING. Charlie Munger Destroys Fake Gurus.

AFTERWORD

"If you take the modern world where people are trying to teach you how to come in and trade actively in stocks—well, I regard that as roughly equivalent to trying to induce a bunch of young people to start off on heroin. It is really stupid. And when you're already rich, to make your money by encouraging people to get rich by trading?

Then there are people on TV—another wonderful place—saying, "I have this book that will teach you how to make 300% a year. All you have to do is pay for shipping, and I'll mail it to you." How likely is it that someone who has suddenly found a way to make 300% a year would be trying to sell books on the internet? It's ridiculous. And yet, I've just described modern commerce, and the people who do this all day think they're useful citizens. The advertising agents invent the lingo."

I think what Charlie Munger is basically getting at is that encouraging people, especially young or inexperienced ones, to dive into active trading is not just irresponsible—it's like leading them into a bad habit they can't shake. He also jokes about how unlikely it is that someone who's found a way to make 300% a year would waste time selling books or courses online. If they really had such a winning strategy, why would they bother? The whole thing just highlights how sketchy modern business can be, from the over-the-top promises to the flashy marketing, and it makes you wonder whether these so-called *experts* are really doing anyone any good.

Interestingly, I have a similar story to tell as well. I know people who've built real estate empires by playing the system—taking on loads of debt and using loopholes to leverage their investments. They would take out multiple bank loans on the same property, pull out extra funds, and use that money to cover loan payments and buy even more properties. Sound familiar, like a popular scheme? Besides, they would also market themselves as investment gurus, showing off fancy cars and luxury homes on social media. But here's the kicker: most of those assets still belong to the banks. Their "students" end up paying thousands for courses, only to find themselves deep in the same cycle—saddled with debt, claiming to own multiple properties without mentioning the liabilities. These so-

AFTERWORD

called gurus may seem "rich," but if they truly are, why do you think they're busy selling courses?

As one might imagine, the same kind of hustle has made its way into the crypto world. You'll run into plenty of self-proclaimed *gurus* pushing flashy get-rich-quick strategies. These folks love to position themselves as experts who've made a killing trading crypto. To draw you in, they'll dangle promises of revealing their so-called secrets, usually kicking things off with a free webinar or some "exclusive" educational content. But here's the kicker: if you want the *real* inside scoop, there's almost always a price tag attached—a pretty steep one.

Additionally, there are also plenty of trading bots marketed as magic money-makers that promise huge returns with minimal effort. You'll see ads hyping up how these bots are expertly programmed to rake in consistent profits, making it sound like an easy ticket to wealth. But think about it: if these bots were really that amazing, why would the people behind them be hustling so hard to advertise and sell them? Wouldn't they just be using the bots themselves and quietly making a killing? It's one of those cases where, if it sounds too good to be true, it probably is.

Lastly, I have one final thought to share. Have you ever considered that one person's wealth often comes at the expense of someone else? In many cases, for someone to get rich, others have to give up their well-being or opportunities. It's a harsh truth: when some people win big, others inevitably lose, and this cycle often leaves people hurt or struggling, and honestly, I'm not sure if there's even a simple solution to that.

What I'm trying to say is that if we're claiming to be building something better, then wealth-building in the crypto space should be about creating real opportunities for everyone—not exploiting those who are just trying to understand. Similarly, when we talk about Bitcoin and cryptocurrencies as the fix for our broken financial systems, shouldn't we make sure we're actually living up to those promises?

AFTERWORD

Otherwise, aren't we just repeating the same mistakes that traditional finance has made? If we believe in the ideals of decentralization, transparency, and financial inclusion, then we have to walk the talk. That means supporting each other, sharing knowledge, and being transparent about the risks as well as the rewards. It's about building a community where people aren't misled or manipulated, but empowered to make informed decisions.

Imagine a crypto space that prioritizes ethical practices and genuinely seeks to uplift everyone involved. What would that look like? Maybe it means calling out scams when we see them, or being more honest about the realities of trading and investing. Maybe it's about mentoring newcomers, or creating resources that actually help people understand the technology rather than just promising them riches. In the end, the real promise of crypto lies not just in financial gains, but in the chance to create a fairer and more inclusive system for all. So, what do you say—are you ready to be part of that change?

PS: Will Bob and Alice's paths cross again? Well, that's a mystery left for you to imagine.

Author Biography

I am a semi-retired engineer who is curious about the ways technology reshapes our understanding of money. Now living a quieter life and pursuing personal projects. It all started in 2017 when I first stumbled into the world of crypto. Like early explorers charting unknown territories, I faced my fair share of challenges. My initial excitement was driven more by curiosity than knowledge, and, naturally, I fell victim to a few scams and failed ventures. Looking back, there is plenty I would have done differently. Now, I just hope to share some honest reflections on the journey, in the hope that it helps others find their way a little more smoothly.

Made in United States
Orlando, FL
06 December 2024